COURSE 2

Practice Workbook

ISBN 0-13-435420-6

Printed in the United States of America.

14   04 03

Editorial Services: Visual Education Corporation

PRENTICE HALL

Table of Contents

Answers to Practice Worksheets appear in the Teacher's Edition and in the back of each Chapter Support File.

Practice 1-1 Reporting Frequency

Make a line plot for the data.

1. boxes of juice sold per day:

   26 21 26 24 27 23 24 22
   26 21 23 26 24 26 23

Ms. Makita made a line plot to show the scores her students got on a test. At the right is Ms. Makita's line plot.

2. What does each data item or ✗ represent?

   _____

3. How many more students scored 75 than scored 95?

   _____

4. How many students scored over 85? _____

5. What scores did the same number of students get?

   _____

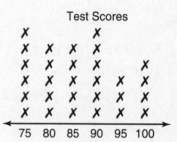

Nathan asked 24 classmates to estimate the total number of hours (to the nearest quarter hour) they spend doing homework Monday through Thursday. The frequency table below shows their responses.

6. Can you tell from the table how many students do homework for two hours or less? Explain. _____

   _____

7. How many more students do homework for at least 5 h than do homework for less than 4 h? _____

8. Make a histogram for the data. Use the intervals in the table.

Hours Spent Doing Homework

Number of Hours	Frequency
1 – 1.75	1
2 – 2.75	1
3 – 3.75	2
4 – 4.75	6
5 – 5.75	8
6 – 6.75	3
7 – 7.75	2
8 – 8.75	1

■■■■Practice 1-2 *Making Bar and Line Graphs*

Would you use a line graph or a bar graph to display each of the following? Explain.

1. the number of Sandburg Middle School graduates in 1990, 1991, 1992, and 1993

   _____

2. the number of students who are the oldest child in their family in each grade at the Emerson Middle School

   _____

   _____

3. Make a line graph of the number of teachers in the school district using the data below.

   Teachers in School District

Year	Number of Teachers
1990	425
1991	430
1992	420
1993	410

4. Estimate the number of teachers in 1994.

   _____

5. Make a bar graph that shows the numbers of seventh-grade students with the given numbers of siblings (brothers and sisters).

   How Many Siblings Do You Have?

Number of Siblings	Number of Students
0	4
1	6
2	5
3	3
4	1
5 or more	1

Survey your classmates about one of the following topics: time spent watching TV last weekend, number of books read last month, color of hair, distance from home to school, or some other topic. Show all your work on a separate sheet of paper.

6. Show the results in a table.

7. Show the results in a graph.

Practice 1-3 *Spreadsheets and Data Displays*

Use the spreadsheet at the right for Exercises 1–4.

1. What is the value in cell B3?

   _____

2. Which cell shows 65 tickets sold?

   _____

Tickets Sold to Concert Performances

	A	B	C
1	Performance	Adult Tickets	Student Tickets
2	Thursday	47	65
3	Friday	125	133
4	Saturday	143	92

3. How many more adult tickets than student tickets were sold on Saturday? _____

4. The concert producer thought she would have the greatest attendance on Saturday. Compare the data with her expectation. _____

   _____

   _____

Decide whether a double bar graph or a double line graph is more appropriate for the given data. Draw the graph.

5. students taking foreign language classes

Year	Boys	Girls
1990	45	60
1991	50	55
1992	70	60
1993	55	75

6. extracurricular sport activities

Sport	Boys	Girls
basketball	40	30
volleyball	30	40
soccer	40	25

▄▄▄ *Practice 1-4* Mean, Median, and Mode

The sum of the heights of all the students in Mrs. Maloney's class is 1,472 in.

1. The mean height is 5 ft 4 in. How many students are in the class? (1 ft = 12 in.) _____

2. The median height is 5 ft 2 in. How many students in Mrs. Maloney's class are 5 ft 2 in. or taller? _____

   How many are shorter? _____

The number of pages read (to the nearest multiple of 50) by the students in Mr. Sullivan's class last week are shown in the tally table at the right.

Pages	Tally
50	I
100	
150	II
200	ʬ I
250	I
300	ʬ
350	III
400	IIII
450	I
500	I

3. Find the mean, the median, and the mode of the data.

   _____

4. What is the outlier in this set of data? _____

5. Does the outlier raise or lower the mean? _____

6. Would you use the mean, median, or mode to most accurately reflect the typical number of pages read by a student?

   Explain. _____

   _____

Kenny hopes to have a 9-point average on his math quizzes. His quiz scores are 7, 6, 10, 8, and 9. Each quiz is worth 12 points.

7. What is Kenny's average quiz score?

   _____

8. There are two more quizzes. How many more points does Kenny need to have a 9-point quiz average? _____

9. Write the numbers from 1 to 6 on slips of paper. Place the numbers in a paper bag or an envelope. Draw out a number 20 times, each time replacing the number before drawing again. Complete the tally table. Find the mean, median, and mode.

   _____

   _____

   _____

Number	Tally
1	_____
2	_____
3	_____
4	_____
5	_____
6	_____

Practice 1-5 *Stem-and-Leaf Plots*

The stem-and-leaf plot at the right shows the number of baskets scored by one of ten intramural teams last season. Use the stem-and-leaf plot for Exercises 1–5.

1. How many data items are there? _____

2. What is the least measurement given? _____

3. What is the greatest measurement given? _____

4. In how many games did the team score less than 70 baskets? _____

5. Find the mean, median, mode, and range. _____

```
5 | 2  6  9
6 | 0  4  6
7 | 1  5
8 | 4  8
```

8|4 means 84

The stem-and-leaf plot at the right shows the number of pages read for book reports by a 7th grade literature class. Use the stem-and-leaf plot for Exercises 6–9.

6. What numbers make up the stems?

_____

7. What numbers make up the leaves for the first stem?

_____

8. How many students read at least 200 pages? _____

9. Find the mean, median, mode, and range. _____

```
19 | 0  5  5
20 | 0  5  9  9
21 | 6
22 | 5  6  8
23 | 2  5  8  8  8
24 | 0  0  4  6
25 | 0  5  5  7  9
```

25|0 means 250

10. Use the data below to create a stem-and-leaf plot. Find the mean, median, mode, and range of the data.

   science test scores: 83   73   78   60   85
                                       92   95   85   99   68

◼◼◼Practice 1-6 *Problem-Solving Strategy:*
Use Logical Reasoning

Use logical reasoning to solve each problem. Show your work.

1. Alicia, Barb, Cathy, Dahlia, and Ellen each arrive at school in a different way. One rides in a car pool, one rides her bike, one walks every day, one rides in her family car, and one rides the school bus. Cathy does not ride in a motor vehicle. Barb enjoys the bus ride along the country road. Ellen is last to be picked up on the car pool route. Alicia lives across the street from school. How does each of the girls arrive at school?

   _____

   _____

2. The top four cross-country runners crossed the finish line as follows. Susan came in after Mary. Donna came in before Susan but did not win the race. Genevieve was last to finish. What was the order of the winners?

   _____

Use any strategy to solve each problem. Show your work.

3. Nick took some money from his piggy bank. He bought a book for $3.50 and he earned $3.00 for raking leaves. Now he has $4.50. How much did Nick take from his bank? _____

4. Find the median of all positive odd multiples of 3 that are less than 50. _____

5. How many different ways can you have $1 in change using nickels, dimes, quarters, and half-dollars? _____

6. Which number shown at the right is described below?

   The difference of the digits is 3.
   It is a multiple of 3.
   It is greater than the average of 84 and 41.
   It is less than the product of 9 and 11.

   It is even. _____

   85   41
   52   74   69
   30   96

Theodore works for Mr. Jonas. Mr. Jonas agreed to start Theodore at $.01 the first day, $.02 the second day, $.04 the third day, $.08 the fourth day, and so on.

7. How much does Theodore earn on the fifteenth day? _____

8. How much did Theodore earn in fifteen days? _____

9. Markie, Bernard, Lyssa, and Hermann entered a race. How many different ways can they finish the race? _____

Practice 1-7 *Random Samples and Surveys*

You want to survey students in your school about their exercise habits. Tell whether the following will give you a random sample. Justify your answer.

1. You select every tenth student on an alphabetical list of the students in your school. You survey the selected students in their first-period classes.

   _____

   _____

2. At lunchtime you stand by a vending machine. You survey every student who buys something from the vending machine.

   _____

   _____

Tell whether the following questions are biased or fair. Rewrite biased questions as fair questions.

3. Do you think bike helmets should be mandatory for all bike riders? _____

4. Do you prefer the natural beauty of hardwood floors in your home? _____

5. Do you exercise regularly? _____

6. Do you eat at least the recommended number of servings of fruits and vegetables to ensure a healthy and long life?

   _____

7. Do you prefer the look and feel of thick lush carpeting in your living room? _____

8. Do you take a daily multiple vitamin to supplement your diet?

   _____

9. Do you read the newspaper to be informed about world events?

   _____

10. Do you feel that the TV news is a sensational portrayal of life's problems? _____

▉▉▉ *Practice 1-8* Using Data to Persuade

The table at the right shows the number of students enrolled in swimming classes for 1991 to 1993.

Swim Class Enrollment		
	Boys	**Girls**
1991	375	360
1992	400	395
1993	410	420

1. Use the data to create a double line graph that emphasizes the increase in the number of students enrolled in summer swim classes.

2. Use the data again to create a second double line graph that does not emphasize the increase in the number of students enrolled in the summer swim classes.

3. Which graph could be used to request additional reserved times for swim classes at the pool? _____

   _____

   _____

Vince has the following scores on chapter tests in his math class. Use this data in Exercises 4–6.

   95   89   83   90   83

4. Find the mean, median, and mode of his test scores.

   _____

5. Should Vince describe his tests using the mean, median, or mode to show his ability to do well in math? _____

   _____

6. Should his teacher use the mean, the median, or the mode to encourage Vince to check his work carefully on the next test?

   _____

▰▰▰ Practice 1-9 *Exploring Scatter Plots*

Tell what trend you would expect to see in scatter plots comparing the following sets of data. Explain your reasoning.

1. a person's height and the person's shoe size _____

   _____

   _____

2. the age of a child and amount of weekly allowance that the child receives _____

   _____

3. the distance one lives from school and the length of the school day _____

   _____

4. the average number of hours a child sleeps and the age of the child

   _____

   _____

5. Make a scatter plot of the following data. Does the scatter plot show any trend? If so, what? _____

Number of Hours of Practice	Number of Successful Free Throws out of 10
6	3
7	5
8	6
9	6
10	7
11	7
12	6
13	7

6. **Circle A, B, or C.** Which of the following scatter plots below probably compares the temperature and the number of people at the toboggan slide?

   A.

   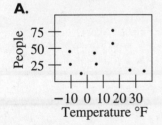

   B.

   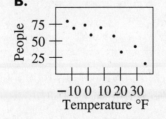

   C.

   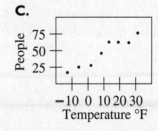

■■■■ Practice 2-1 *Comparing and Rounding Decimals*

Write five numbers between the given numbers. List the numbers in order from least to greatest.

1. 30 and 35

2. 55 and 60

3. 15 and 17

4. 43 and 45

5. 8 and 9

6. 19 and 20

7. 1.3 and 1.4

8. 2.6 and 2.65

Identify the place value of the underlined digit. Then round each decimal to the indicated place.

9. 0.82$\underline{7}$65

10. 8.$\underline{7}$59

11. 4.3$\underline{2}$457

12. 7.0$\underline{0}$92

13. 0.7$\underline{1}$99

14. 0.090$\underline{9}$9

15. 5.123$\underline{5}$79

16. 2.4$\underline{5}$9

17. 5.00$\underline{2}$3

18. 4.0$\underline{2}$39

19. 0.0102$\underline{0}$6

20. 7.999905

Compare using <, >, or =.

21. 0.23 ☐ 0.230

22. 4.79 ☐ 4.8

23. 1.92 ☐ 1.09

24. 5.72 ☐ 5.3

25. 4.706 ☐ 4.71

26. 22.6 ☐ 22.60

27. 8.09 ☐ 8.90

28. 0.003 ☐ 2.0030

29. 1.023 ☐ 1.203

30. 10.4 ☐ 10.41

31. 0.41 ☐ 0.14

32. 4.390 ☐ 4.3900

33. Write 5 decimals that round to 0.96. _____

_____

34. Each year, the North American continent moves approximately 1.2 in. farther away from Europe. Write three possible measurements that round to 1.2 in. _____

_____

35. The length of each day of the year changes by about 0.00000002 s. Write a length of time that could be rounded up to this figure.

_____

■■■■Practice 2-2 Problem Solving:
Using Estimation Strategies

Estimate by rounding to the nearest half-dollar.

1. $4.85
    + 1.47
    _____

2. $6.79
    − 3.95
    _____

3. $14.19
    + 5.59
    _____

4. $25.43
    − 21.20
    _____

Use front-end estimation to find each sum.

5. 4.76 + 6.15

6. 1.409 + 3.512

7. 2.479 + 6.518

8. 3.17 + 2.72

9. 9.87 + 2.16

10. 5.89 + 7.21

Use clustering to estimate each sum.

11. 8.9 + 9.01 + 9.3 + 8.7 + 9.15

12. 5.7 + 6.3 + 5.9 + 6.12 + 5.87

13. $24.79 + $25.79 + $25.02 + $24.10 + $25.19 + $24.59

14. $66.93 + $72.18 + $69.18 + $71.94 + $65.75

Use any estimation strategy to calculate. Tell which strategy you used.

15. 93.26 − 69.78

16. 51.12 × 87.906

17. 43.19 + 26.87

18. 457.03 + 592.8

19. 702 ÷ 61

20. 81.19 × 38.69

21. 12.87 + 14.31 + 15.09

22. 536 ÷ 41

23. 526.89 − 417.26

Find each estimate.

24. A rare truffle once sold for $13.20 for a 0.44 oz can. Approximately how much would 1 lb of this truffle cost?

25. The longest loaf of bread measured 1,405 ft $1\frac{3}{4}$ in. in length. It was cut into slices $\frac{1}{2}$ in. thick. How many slices were there?

▅▅▅▅*Practice 2-3* Adding and Subtracting Decimals

Identify each property shown in the equation.

1. $(8.7 + 6.3) + 3.7 = 8.7 + (6.3 + 3.7)$ **2.** $9.06 + 0 = 9.06$

_____   _____

3. $4.06 + 8.92 = 8.92 + 4.06$ **4.** $0 + 7.13 = 7.13 + 0$

_____   _____

5. $(8.4 + 12.6) + 4.7 = 8.4 + (12.6 + 4.7)$ **6.** $0 + 17.96 - 17.96$

_____   _____

Find each sum.

7. $4.6 + 8.79$ **8.** $14.8 + 29.07$ **9.** $20.16 + 15.703$

10. $36.12 + 5.793$ **11.** $8.9 + 2.14 + 7.1$ **12.** $3.6 + 5.27 + 8.93$

13. $107.5 + 6$ **14.** $15.26 + 13.29 + 38.96$ **15.** $46.21 + 53.942$

16. $83.14 + 96.72$ **17.** $58.01 + 74.94$ **18.** $9 + 0.638$

Find each difference.

19. $8.7 - 2.03$ **20.** $53.86 - 4.02$ **21.** $14.59 - 8.3$ **22.** $27.13 - 18.9$

23. $42.75 - 26.36$ **24.** $53.86 - 16.47$ **25.** $56.89 - 48.91$ **26.** $23.5 - 18.079$

27. $5.06 - 3.297$ **28.** $3.4 - 2.768$ **29.** $5.002 - 4.3$ **30.** $0.2406 - 0.058$

Use the advertisement at the right. Find each cost.

31. 1 egg _____

32. toast _____

33. bacon _____

2 eggs, toast, bacon, milk	$2.75
1 egg, toast, bacon, milk	$2.20
toast, milk	$0.90
toast, bacon, milk	$1.65
1 egg, toast	$0.95

34. milk _____

35. 1 egg and milk _____

36. 1 egg and bacon _____

■■■■*Practice 2-4* Problem-Solving Strategy:
Too Much or Too Little Information

**Use any strategy to solve each problem. If it is not possible
to solve, tell what needed information is missing.**

1. Mary Jo wants to buy some stamps and three envelopes. Envelopes cost $.10 each, and stamps cost $.29 each. How much will the stamps and envelopes cost?

2. Royce earns $200 per week, plus $50 for every stereo system that he sells. Last week, he earned $850. How many stereo systems did Royce sell last week?

3. Four friends were standing in the lunch line. Tom was not last. Hank was in line immediately after Cindy. Tom and Beverly had at least one person between them. In what order were the four standing?

4. A store had a grand-opening sale on Friday and Saturday. Over 400 people attended on Friday, and four times as many people attended on Saturday. If each person attending had to buy a ticket to enter, how many tickets were needed?

5. You have a set of models of two-dimensional shapes. A balance scale balances with one triangle and three squares on one side, and one square, two circles, and one triangle on the other side. Each triangle weighs 2 kg. Each square weighs 3 kg. How much does each circle weigh?

6. Rodrigo wants to double a recipe requiring 1 c milk and 3 c flour. How much cinnamon should he add?

7. The Smythe children take turns picking which TV show to watch. Jo picks first since she is the youngest. Lyle picks immediately before Mark. Meg picks before Beth, but after Lyle. In what order do the children pick which TV show to watch?

8. The Hsu family pays $15 per month for trash pickup, plus $7 per large item. How much did they pay for trash pickup last year if they got rid of an old couch and a refrigerator?

▄▄▄▄ *Practice 2-5* Multiplying Decimals

Use a model, paper and pencil, or a calculator to find each product.

1. 28×6 **2.** $7.3 \cdot 0.9$ **3.** $58 \cdot 2.1$ **4.** $15(187)$

_____   _____   _____   _____

5. 6.6×25 **6.** $(1.8)(0.7)$ **7.** $0.91 \cdot 2.7$ **8.** $4.6(3.9)$

_____   _____   _____   _____

Rewrite each equation with the decimal point in the correct place in the product.

9. $5.6 \times 1.2 = 672$ **10.** $3.7 \times 2.4 = 888$ **11.** $6.5 \times 2.5 = 1625$

_____   _____   _____

12. $1.02 \times 6.9 = 7038$ **13.** $4.4 \times 6.51 = 28644$ **14.** $0.6 \times 9.312 = 55872$

_____   _____   _____

Name the property of multiplication shown.

15. $3 \times 4 = 4 \times 3$ **16.** $9 \times (6 \times 3) = (9 \times 6) \times 3$

_____   _____

17. $2 \times 0 = 0$ **18.** $10 \times 1 = 10$

_____   _____

Use mental math and the properties of multiplication to find the value of each expression.

19. $0.4 \times 6.71 \times 5$ **20.** $8.3 \times 2.1 \times 0 \times 4.6$ **21.** $5.9 \times 0.3 \times 10$

_____   _____   _____

22. $(5.3 \times 2.5) \times 4$ **23.** $0.3 \times 6.21 \times 10$ **24.** $(7.5 \times 9.3) \times 4$

_____   _____   _____

Solve.

25. Al's Car Rental charges $122.50 for a 5-day rental and then $27.50 for each additional day. Dave's Car Rental charges a flat rate of $26.25 per day. Which company charges less for a 7-day car rental? _____

26. Anitta works in a department store and earns $7.60 per hour. Last week she worked 39.5 hours. How much money did she earn for the week? _____

▪▪▪ *Practice 2-6* *Dividing Decimals*

Circle A, B, or C. Estimate each quotient. Choose the best answer.

1. $10 \div 4.6$ **A.** 0.23   **B.** 2.3   **C.** 33

2. $9.9 \div 2.7$ **A.** 40   **B.** 4   **C.** 0.37

3. $43.68 \div 7.8$ **A.** 6   **B.** 60   **C.** 0.56

4. $65.29 \div 8.5$ **A.** 80   **B.** 72   **C.** 8

Use mental math to find each quotient.

5. $0.7 \div 100$ **6.** $4.85 \div 0.1$ **7.** $7.08 \div 10$ **8.** $3.5 \div 0.1$

9. $847 \div 0.01$ **10.** $0.3 \div 0.1$ **11.** $32.6 \div 0.01$ **12.** $5.02 \div 0.1$

Choose mental math, paper and pencil, or a calculator.

13. $2.1\overline{)12.6}$ **14.** $29.75 \div 0.7$ **15.** $37 \div 0.2$ **16.** $4.74 \div 0.06$

17. $1.414 \div 1.4$ **18.** $0.78\overline{)0.16614}$ **19.** $0.154 \div 5.5$ **20.** $0.85\overline{)0.0527}$

Find each quotient. Check each answer.

21. $42.6 \div 6$ **22.** $3\overline{)6.51}$ **23.** $106.4 \div 7$ **24.** $8\overline{)31.2}$

25. $81.648 \div 14$ **26.** $55.68 \div 32$ **27.** $9\overline{)7.704}$ **28.** $7.518 \div 15$

Solve.

29. Alicia paid $1.32 for a bag of pinto beans. The beans cost $0.55 per lb. How much did the bag of pinto beans weigh?

30. Nina and 3 friends ate lunch at a cafe. They decided to split the bill evenly. The total bill was $17.84. How much was each person's share?

■■■Practice 2-7 _Terminating and Repeating Decimals_

Write each repeating decimal using a bar.

1. 0.333 . . .   **2.** 0.125125 . . .   **3.** 0.8787 . . .   **4.** 3.5666 . . .

_____   _____   _____   _____

5. 0.030030 . . .   **6.** 7.322322 . . .   **7.** 5.7745353 . . .   **8.** 12.11222 . . .

_____   _____   _____   _____

Write each repeating decimal without a bar.

9. $0.\overline{5}$ **10.** $0.7\overline{32}$ **11.** $5.8\overline{218}$ **12.** $7.\overline{56}$

_____   _____   _____   _____

13. $0.9\overline{7}$ **14.** $0.\overline{003}$ **15.** $8.2\overline{11}$ **16.** $24.\overline{48}$

_____   _____   _____   _____

Use a calculator to find each answer.

17. $1 \div 2 + 9 \div 6$ **18.** $5 \div 3 + 32 \div 12$ **19.** $15 \div 9 - 24 \div 18$

_____   _____   _____

20. $2 \div 14 + 10 \div 28$ **21.** $10 \div 8 - 3 \div 24$ **22.** $9 \div 13 - 27 \div 39$

_____   _____   _____

23. $35 \div 10 + 18 \div 12$ **24.** $9 \div 11 - 7 \div 22$ **25.** $7 \div 4 + 24 \div 40$

_____   _____   _____

Choose a calculator or paper and pencil to find each quotient. Use a bar to show repeating decimals.

26. $5 \div 8$ **27.** $7 \div 8$ **28.** $9 \div 16$ **29.** $7 \div 16$

_____   _____   _____   _____

30. $4 \div 9$ **31.** $5 \div 32$ **32.** $7 \div 12$ **33.** $11 \div 32$

_____   _____   _____   _____

34. $5 \div 4$ **35.** $5 \div 7$ **36.** $2 \div 11$ **37.** $4 \div 7$

_____   _____   _____   _____

38. $6 \div 13$ **39.** $11 \div 3$ **40.** $8 \div 9$ **41.** $11 \div 9$

_____   _____   _____   _____

42. $7 \div 32$ **43.** $9 \div 32$ **44.** $5 \div 16$ **45.** $8 \div 15$

_____   _____   _____   _____

Practice 3-2 Comparing and Ordering Integers

Name the integer represented by each point on the number line.

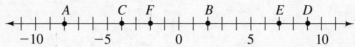

1. A ____   **2.** B ____   **3.** C ____   **4.** D ____   **5.** E ____   **6.** F ____

Compare. Use <, >, or =.

7. −8 ☐ 8   **8.** 4 ☐ −4   **9.** |5| ☐ |−5| **10.** −8 ☐ 0

11. −6 ☐ −2   **12.** −1 ☐ −3   **13.** |−4| ☐ 0   **14.** |−3| ☐ 2

Graph each integer and its opposite on the number line.

15. −9

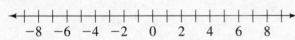

16. 5

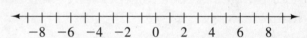

17. 6

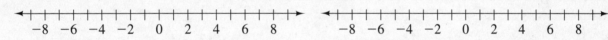

18. 7

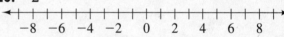

19. 8

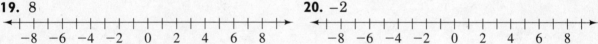

20. −2

Find the value of each expression.

21. |2| **22.** |−3| **23.** |−38| **24.** |−2 + 5| **25.** |−44|

_____   _____   _____   _____   _____

26. |5| + 4   **27.** |−5| + 4   **28.** |5 + 2| **29.** |−16| **30.** |3 − 7|

_____   _____   _____   _____   _____

Write an integer to represent each situation.

31. A gain of 5 yards   **32.** A debt of $5   **33.** 4 degrees below zero

_____   _____   _____

34. A temperature of 100°F   **35.** 135 feet below sea level   **36.** A loss of $30

_____   _____   _____

■■■Practice 3-3 *Using Models: Adding Integers*

Group zero pairs. Then write the addition equation for each model.

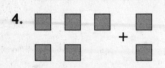

1. □ □ + ■ ■
   □ □   ■ ■
_____

2. ■ ■ + ■ ■
   ■   ■ ■
_____

3. □ □ □ □ + ■
   □ □ □   □
_____

4. ■ ■ ■ ■ + ■
   ■ ■   ■
_____

5. ■ ■ □ +
   ■ ■ □
_____

6. □ □ □ □ + ■ ■
   □ □ □ □   ■ ■
_____

Find each sum.

7. $-2 + (-3)$ **8.** $8 - 7 + 4$ **9.** $8 + (-5)$ **10.** $15 + (-3)$

_____   _____   _____   _____

11. $-16 + 8$ **12.** $7 + (-10)$ **13.** $-9 + (-5)$ **14.** $-12 + 14$

_____   _____   _____   _____

Sketch algebra tiles to represent each number in two different ways.

15. 1   **16.** 3   **17.** -2

Simplify each expression using mental math.

18. $3 + 8 + (-4)$ **19.** $2 + |-3| + (-3)$ **20.** $9 + 7 + (-6)$

_____   _____   _____

21. $56 + (-4) + (-58)$ **22.** $-4 + 3 + (-2)$ **23.** $|-8| + 15 + (-8)$

_____   _____   _____

Use absolute values to find each sum.

24. $43 + (-40)$ **25.** $-12 + 12$ **26.** $-25 + 16$ **27.** $53 + (-33)$

_____   _____   _____   _____

28. $127 + (-83)$ **29.** $54 + (-96)$ **30.** $-87 + (-56)$ **31.** $-152 + 43$

_____   _____   _____   _____

Practice 3-4 Subtracting Integers

Use >, <, or = to complete each statement.

1. −9 − (−11) ☐ 0   **2.** −17 + 20 ☐ 0   **3.** 11 − (−4) ☐ 0   **4.** −19 + 16 ☐ 0

5. 28 − 19 ☐ 0   **6.** 52 + (−65) ☐ 0   **7.** −28 − (−28) ☐ 0   **8.** −28 − (−53) ☐ 0

Choose a calculator, paper and pencil, or mental math to subtract.

9. 9 − 26   **10.** −4 − 15   **11.** 21 − (−7)   **12.** 27 − (−16)

_____   _____   _____   _____

13. −16 − (−43)   **14.** 47 − 19   **15.** −156 − 98   **16.** −192 − 47

_____   _____   _____   _____

17. 0 − (−51)   **18.** −63 − 89   **19.** −12 − (−21)   **20.** 92 − (−16)

_____   _____   _____   _____

21. 72 − 15   **22.** −86 − (−19)   **23.** 17 − (−46)   **24.** −78 − (−53)

_____   _____   _____   _____

Solve.

25. The highest and lowest temperatures ever recorded in Africa are 136°F and −11°F. The highest temperature was recorded in Libya, and the lowest temperature was recorded in Morocco. What is the difference in these temperature extremes? _____

26. The highest and lowest temperatures ever recorded in South America are 120°F and −27°F. Both the highest and lowest temperatures were recorded in Argentina. What is the difference in these temperature extremes? _____

Find each difference. Ignore any negative signs when placing the result in the puzzle.

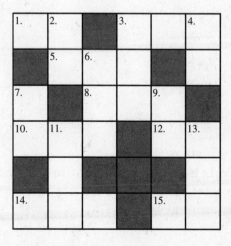

Across	Down
1. 18 − (−8)	**2.** −72 − (−9)
3. −156 − 78	**3.** −125 − 88
5. 451 − 110	**4.** 58 − 11
8. 120 − (−15)	**6.** 592 − 175
10. −450 − 77	**7.** −93 − (−48)
12. −8 − 18	**9.** 126 − 74
14. 128 − (−375)	**11.** −112 − 98
15. 94 − 13	**13.** −102 − (−743)

Course 2 Chapter 3

■■■Practice 3-5 Multiplying and Dividing Integers

Complete each number sentence. Then write two examples
to illustrate each relationship.

1. positive ÷ positive

_____

2. negative · positive

_____

3. positive · positive

_____

4. negative ÷ negative

_____

5. negative ÷ positive

_____

6. positive · positive

_____

7. positive ÷ negative

_____

8. negative · negative

_____

Estimate each product or quotient.

9. $-72 \cdot 57$ **10.** $-92 \cdot (-41)$ **11.** $-476 \div 90$ **12.** $-83 \cdot 52$

_____   _____   _____   _____

13. $538 \div (-63)$ **14.** $-803(-106)$ **15.** $49 \cdot 61$ **16.** $479 \div (-61)$

_____   _____   _____   _____

Use the order of operations to evaluate.

17. $-36 \div 9 + 4(-7)$ **18.** $-52 \div (-4) + (-3)(-6)$ **19.** $-13 + (-5)(-4)$

_____   _____   _____

20. $-8(9) - 4(-7)$ **21.** $-3(7 - 12) - 8$ **22.** $-24(-7 - 12)$

_____   _____   _____

23. $-8(-7) - 12$ **24.** $-15(-8 - 9)$ **25.** $-8(46 - 92) + (-4)$

_____   _____   _____

26. $7(-8 - 5)$ **27.** $-9(-11 + 17)$ **28.** $4(-4 + 7)$

_____   _____   _____

29. $-15(-9 + 6)$ **30.** $43(8 - 9)$ **31.** $83(-7 - 2) - (-4)$

_____   _____   _____

**Find the point on the number line that shows each product
or quotient.**

32. $-4 \cdot 0$ **33.** $12 \div (-3)$ **34.** $(-2) \cdot (-2)$ **35.** $-6 \div 3$ **36.** $1 \cdot (-5)$

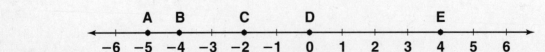

Practice 3-6 Solving Equations by Adding and Subtracting

Solve each equation. Use mental math to check the solution.

1. $n + 2 = 5$ **2.** $x - 1 = -3$ **3.** $7 = a + 2$ **4.** $p + 2 = -6$

_____   _____   _____   _____

5. $-9 = -4 + a$ **6.** $-2 = c + 2$ **7.** $x - (-3) = 7$ **8.** $a + (-6) = 5$

_____   _____   _____   _____

9. $10 = r - 5$ **10.** $x + 10 = 2$ **11.** $-5 + c = -1$ **12.** $-12 = 7 + h$

_____   _____   _____   _____

13. $16 + s = 6$ **14.** $p + (-2) = 19$ **15.** $r - 7 = -13$ **16.** $25 = a - (-3)$

_____   _____   _____   _____

Choose a calculator, paper and pencil, or mental math to solve each equation. Check the solution.

17. $t + 43 = 28$ **18.** $-19 = r + 6$ **19.** $25 = r + 7$ **20.** $13 = 24 + c$

_____   _____   _____   _____

21. $d - 19 = -46$ **22.** $b + 27 = -18$ **23.** $46 = f - 19$ **24.** $z - 74 = -19$

_____   _____   _____   _____

Circle A, B, C, or D in Exercises 25 and 26.

25. After driving 62.3 miles, the odometer on Mira's car read 20,186.7. Which equation could you use to find how many miles were on the odometer before driving 62.3 miles?

    A. $20,186.7 + 62.3 = m$ **B.** $m + 20,186.7 = 62.3$
    C. $m + 62.3 = 20,186.7$ **D.** $m - 62.3 = 20,186.7$

26. Michael bought a $25.00 gift for a friend. After he bought the gift, Michael had $176.89. Which equation could you use to find how much money Michael had before he bought the gift?

    A. $g + \$176.89 = \$25.00$ **B.** $g - \$25.00 = \$176.89$
    C. $g + \$25.00 = \$176.89$ **D.** $\$176.89 - \$25.00 = g$

27. In Exercise 25, find the odometer reading before the trip.

_____

28. In Exercise 26, find how much money Michael had before he bought the gift. _____

▬▬▬ Practice 3-7 Solving Equations by
                    Multiplying and Dividing

**Choose a calculator, paper and pencil, or mental math to
solve each equation. Check the solution.**

1. $9n = 126$

2. $\frac{d}{3} = -81$

3. $-2t = 56$

4. $\frac{k}{-3} = 6$

5. $-18 = \frac{y}{-2}$

6. $y \div 16 = 3$

7. $-56 = 8r$

8. $9w = -63$

9. $-3v = -48$

10. $13 = x \div (-4)$

11. $28 = -4a$

12. $t \div (-42) = 3$

13. $-19 = f \div 6$

14. $75 = -5s$

15. $\frac{q}{4} = 56$

16. $18w = -36$

17. $24 = f \div (-4)$

18. $15 = -3j$

19. $102k = 408$

20. $\frac{b}{-96} = -3$

Estimate the solution.

21. $\frac{x}{19} = -21$

22. $\frac{x}{-22} = -63$

23. $-41x = 161$

24. $-98r = 1,200$

25. $\frac{x}{91} = -98$

26. $452 = -4x$

27. $52x = -2,500$

28. $79x = -6,380$

**Write an equation to represent each situation.
Solve the equation.**

29. One of the largest flowers, the Rafflesia, weighs about 15 lb.
How many Rafflesia flowers can be placed in a container that
can hold a maximum of 240 lb?

_____

30. "Heavy water" is a name given to a compound used in some
nuclear reactors. Heavy water costs about $1,500 per gallon.
If a nuclear plant spent $10,500 on heavy water, how many
gallons of heavy water were bought?

_____

Practice 3-8 Writing Equations

Write an equation. Then solve.

1. The sum of 63 and some number is 82.

   _____

2. A number divided by negative 18 is 26.

   _____

3. Nine times a number is 54.

   _____

4. Fifty-two divided by a number equals 4.

   _____

5. A number divided by 8 equals 12.

   _____

6. Sixty-eight is ninety-seven less than a number.

   _____

7. Forty-nine is thirteen less than a number.

   _____

8. Eighty-three times a number is 1,411.

   _____

9. Fifty-seven is 19 more than some number.

   _____

10. Seventy-five times a number is 1,800.

    _____

11. In order to make a teaspoon of honey, a honeybee must make 154 trips. If a honeybee made 924 trips, how many teaspoons of honey could it make?

    _____

12. Eight travelers sleeping in a hostel are snoring. The hostel has 15 sleeping travelers. How many travelers are not snoring?

    _____

13. On a trip, the Rodriguez family drove an average of 250 mi each day. If the family drove a total of 3,000 mi on their trip, how many days were they gone?

    _____

14. Maida has completed typing 6 pages of her term paper. If her term paper is 18 pages long, how many more pages does she have to type?

    _____

15. Hoshi plans to read 500 pages of a book in one week. He has completed 142 pages so far this week. How many more pages must he read?

    _____

16. After withdrawing $58, Martha had $200 left in her savings account. How much money was in the account before the withdrawal?

    _____

▬▬▬Practice 3-9 Solving Two-Step Equations

Solve each equation. Use mental math to check the solution.

1. $7m + 8 = 71$ **2.** $\frac{y}{7} + 6 = 11$ **3.** $12y + 2 = 146$ **4.** $\frac{m}{9} - 17 = 21$

_____ _____ _____ _____

5. $\frac{y}{-12} + 1 = 6$ **6.** $2a - 1 = 19$ **7.** $\frac{c}{9} - 8 = 17$ **8.** $-4t + 16 = 24$

_____ _____ _____ _____

9. $4f + 11 = -29$ **10.** $\frac{g}{17} - 8 = -6$ **11.** $13n - 9 = 17$ **12.** $5v - 42 = 73$

_____ _____ _____ _____

13. $\frac{b}{-2} - 8 = -6$ **14.** $3d + 14 = 11$ **15.** $\frac{z}{17} - 1 = 8$ **16.** $\frac{e}{5} - 14 = 21$

_____ _____ _____ _____

17. $\frac{f}{-9} + 4 = 2$ **18.** $-2y + 16 = 10$ **19.** $4w - 26 = 82$ **20.** $\frac{j}{19} - 2 = -5$

_____ _____ _____ _____

Write a calculator sequence to solve each equation. Then solve.

21. $3n - 8 = 4$ **22.** $\frac{n}{5} - 4 = 11$

_____ _____

23. $2n - 3 = 9$ **24.** $1 + \frac{n}{4} = 9$

_____ _____

Match each sentence with a two-step equation.

25. Half a number minus five equals fifteen. _____

26. Five more than half of a number equals fifteen. _____

27. Two less than three times a number equals twelve. _____

28. Eight less than the quotient of a number and four equals negative five. _____

29. Three times a number increased by two equals twelve. _____

30. Eight fewer than four times a number equals negative five. _____

A. $4n - 8 = -5$

B. $3n - 2 = 12$

C. $\frac{n}{2} + 5 = 15$

D. $3n + 2 = 12$

E. $\frac{n}{2} - 5 = 15$

F. $\frac{n}{4} - 8 = -5$

Practice 3-10 Problem-Solving Strategy: Make a Table

Make a table to solve each problem.

1. At a yard sale, Rhonda bought 9 items costing either $.50 or $.75. If she spent a total of $5.00, how many items of each price did Rhonda buy?

   _____

2. You have a penny, a nickel, and a dime. Name the different amounts of money that are possible using one or more of these coins.

   _____

3. Vijay bought 11 tickets for a waterslide. The tickets were $6 for adults and $4 for children. Vijay paid $60 for the tickets. For how many adults and how many children did he buy tickets?

   _____

4. A certain kind of sports car is available in red, white, black, or silver. The upholstery is available in leather, vinyl, or cloth. The dealer keeps one of each possible type on the lot. How many sports cars are on the lot?

   _____

Use any strategy to solve each problem. Show all your work.

5. Over the summer three friends saved a total of $180. Marti saved twice as much as Paula and $10 more than Oscar. How much did each save?

   _____

6. Find two integers whose sum is 5 and whose product is −36.

   _____

7. A ball is dropped from a height of 16 ft. Each time it hits the ground it bounces three-fourths of its previous height. The ball is caught when the height of its bounce is $6\frac{3}{4}$ ft. What is the total vertical distance the ball traveled?

   _____

8. Mai and Juan are friends. They live at corners of the blocks as shown below. How many different routes can Juan take to Mai's house? He only travels west or north and does not retrace his steps.

   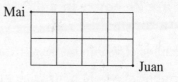

   _____

9. How many rectangles are in the figure below?

   _____

▬▬ *Practice 4-1* Relating Fractions to Models

Write a fraction for each model.

1. 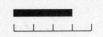 ____

2. ____

3. 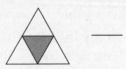 ____

Write a mixed number for each model.

4.  ____

5.  ____

6.  ____

Write the fraction or a mixed number represented by the shaded parts.

7. ____

8. ____

9.  ____

10. One brand of cheese comes in packages of 12 slices. Anna used 7 slices for grilled cheese sandwiches.

   a. What part of the package did she use? ____

   b. What part of the package was left over? ____

There are 24 hours in a day. For Exercises 11–14, write the fraction for each.

11. number of whole hours you slept last night   _____

12. number of whole hours you spent at school today   _____

13. number of whole hours you spend doing homework   _____

14. number of whole hours you spend watching TV   _____

15. What part of the alphabet consists of vowels?   _____

16. Use your first name. Write a fraction for the part of your name made of vowels. Write a fraction for the part of your name made of consonants.

Practice 4-2 Equivalent Fractions

1. **a.** Write the first five multiples of 6 and 9. _____

   b. What is the smallest multiple that 6 and 9 have in common? _____

2. **a.** Write the factors of 6 and the factors of 9. _____

   b. What factors do 6 and 9 have in common? _____

Match each fraction in the column on the left with its equivalent in the column on the right.

3. $\frac{3}{8}$ _____ A. $\frac{3}{5}$

4. $\frac{7}{12}$ _____ B. $\frac{7}{8}$

5. $\frac{6}{10}$ _____ C. $\frac{6}{12}$

6. $\frac{14}{16}$ _____ D. $\frac{5}{6}$

7. $\frac{1}{2}$ _____ E. $\frac{21}{28}$

8. $\frac{3}{4}$ _____ F. $\frac{14}{24}$

9. $\frac{2}{3}$ _____ G. $\frac{14}{21}$

10. $\frac{25}{30}$ _____ H. $\frac{9}{24}$

11. Name two fractions that are modeled.

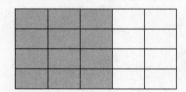

_____

Find the number that makes a true statement.

12. $\frac{10}{16} = \frac{x}{8}$ _____ 13. $\frac{16}{24} = \frac{2}{x}$ _____ 14. $\frac{15}{25} = \frac{x}{5}$ _____

15. $\frac{21}{35} = \frac{3}{x}$ _____ 16. $\frac{8}{32} = \frac{1}{x}$ _____ 17. $\frac{x}{36} = \frac{7}{9}$ _____

Solve.

18. Which of the following numbers, 2, 3, 4, 5, 6, 8, 9, and 10, are factors of 2,910? _____

19. The Rano family decided to wrap presents together. Kim wrapped three presents for her grandmother. Her mother wrapped two presents. Her sister wrapped one present. What fraction of their grandmother's presents did each family member wrap?

   _____

Practice 4-3 Comparing and Ordering Fractions

Write the two fractions modeled and compare them.

1.

2.

3.

_____   _____   _____

Find the LCD of each pair of fractions.

4. $\frac{5}{8}, \frac{5}{6}$ _____

5. $\frac{5}{12}, \frac{7}{8}$ _____

6. $\frac{9}{10}, \frac{1}{2}$ _____

7. $\frac{2}{3}, \frac{3}{4}$ _____

8. $\frac{1}{6}, \frac{3}{10}$ _____

9. $\frac{1}{4}, \frac{2}{15}$ _____

10. $\frac{5}{6}, \frac{8}{15}$ _____

11. $\frac{7}{12}, \frac{9}{20}$ _____

Compare. Use <, >, or =.

12. $\frac{7}{8} \square \frac{3}{8}$

13. $\frac{4}{5} \square \frac{1}{2}$

14. $\frac{6}{12} \square \frac{4}{8}$

15. $\frac{7}{15} \square \frac{11}{15}$

16. $\frac{4}{5} \square \frac{6}{10}$

17. $\frac{7}{12} \square \frac{2}{3}$

18. $\frac{8}{15} \square \frac{1}{2}$

19. $\frac{10}{15} \square \frac{8}{12}$

20. $\frac{4}{9} \square \frac{7}{9}$

21. $\frac{2}{5} \square \frac{3}{8}$

22. $\frac{1}{2} \square \frac{11}{20}$

23. $\frac{7}{16} \square \frac{1}{2}$

Order from least to greatest.

24. $\frac{1}{4}, \frac{1}{3}, \frac{1}{6}$ _____

25. $\frac{1}{2}, \frac{5}{6}, \frac{7}{8}$ _____

26. $\frac{1}{4}, \frac{2}{5}, \frac{3}{8}$ _____

27. $\frac{7}{8}, \frac{5}{9}, \frac{2}{3}$ _____

28. $\frac{3}{8}, \frac{5}{6}, \frac{1}{2}$ _____

29. $\frac{9}{10}, \frac{11}{12}, \frac{15}{16}$ _____

30. $\frac{3}{4}, \frac{1}{2}, \frac{7}{8}$ _____

31. $\frac{5}{9}, \frac{2}{3}, \frac{7}{12}$ _____

32. $\frac{15}{16}, \frac{7}{8}, \frac{1}{2}$ _____

Solve.

33. A pattern requires a seam of at least $\frac{5}{8}$ in. Rachel sewed a seam $\frac{1}{2}$ in. wide. Did she sew the seam wide enough? Explain.

_____

34. Marc needs $\frac{3}{4}$ c of milk for a recipe. He has $\frac{2}{3}$ c. Does he have enough? Explain.

_____

35. Monica is growing three bean plants as part of a science experiment. Plant A is $\frac{1}{2}$ in. tall. Plant B is $\frac{3}{4}$ in. tall. Plant C is $\frac{3}{8}$ in. tall. Order the plants from shortest to tallest.

_____

36. During a rainstorm Willow received $\frac{7}{16}$ in. of rain and Riverton received $\frac{5}{8}$ in. of rain. Which community received more rain?

_____

Practice 4-4 Exponents and Order of Operations

Write each expression using exponents.

1. $3 \times 3 \times 3 \times 3 \times 3$ _____

2. $2.7 \times 2.7 \times 2.7$ _____

3. $11.6 \times 11.6 \times 11.6 \times 11.6$ _____

4. $2 \times 2 \times 2 \times 2 \times 2 \times 2 \times 2$ _____

5. $8.3 \times 8.3 \times 8.3 \times 8.3 \times 8.3$ _____

6. $4 \times 4 \times 4 \times 4 \times 4 \times 4 \times 4 \times 4$ _____

Write each expression as the product of repeated factors.
Then evaluate each expression.

7. 0.5^3 _____

8. 4^5 _____

9. 2.7^2 _____

10. 2^3 _____

11. 5^6 _____

12. 8.1^3 _____

Choose a calculator, paper and pencil, or mental math to evaluate each expression.

13. -4^3

14. $8^3 + 9$

15. $11 + 6^3$

16. $14 + 16^2$

17. $8 + 6^4$

18. $2^5 + 2^3$

19. $3^2 \cdot 5^4$

20. $6^2 - 2^4$

21. $4 (0.9 + 1.3)^3$

22. $3 (1.5 - 0.2)^3$

23. $3^5 - (4^2 + 5)$

24. $(3^3 + 6) - 7$

25. $5 (0.3 \cdot 1.2)^2$

26. $18 \div (1.4 - 0.4)^2$

27. $5 (4 + 2)^2$

28. $(8 - 6.7)^3$

Circle A, B, or C.

29. $2^4 \blacksquare 4^2$

    A. $>$ **B.** $<$ **C.** $=$

30. $3^6 \blacksquare 6^3$

    A. $>$ **B.** $<$ **C.** $=$

31. $2^5 \blacksquare 5^2$

    A. $>$ **B.** $<$ **C.** $=$

▬▬▬*Practice 4-5* Prime Factorization

Determine whether each number is prime or composite.

1. 97 _____   **2.** 63 _____   **3.** 29 _____   **4.** 120 _____

Use a factor tree to find the prime factors of each number. Then write the prime factorization, using exponents where possible.

5. 42 _____   **6.** 130 _____   **7.** 78 _____   **8.** 126 _____

9. 125 _____   **10.** 90 _____   **11.** 92 _____   **12.** 180 _____

Use a calculator to find the number with the given prime factorization.

13. $3^2 \cdot 11^2$ _____   **14.** $2^2 \cdot 3 \cdot 5^3$ _____   **15.** $3^2 \cdot 5^2 \cdot 7^3$ _____

Make lists of factors for each set of numbers. Then find the GCF.

16. 16, 20   _____   _____   _____

17. 24, 30   _____   _____   _____

18. 10, 25   _____   _____   _____

19. 15, 24   _____   _____   _____

Find the GCF for each pair of numbers.

20. 45, 60 _____   **21.** 18, 42 _____   **22.** 32, 80 _____

23. 20, 65 _____   **24.** 24, 90 _____   **25.** 17, 34 _____

26. 14, 35 _____   **27.** 51, 27 _____   **28.** 42, 63 _____

◼️ **Practice 4-6** *Simplifying Fractions*

Write each fraction in simplest form.

1. $\frac{8}{12}$ ____

2. $\frac{9}{15}$ ____

3. $\frac{16}{20}$ ____

4. $\frac{20}{25}$ ____

5. $\frac{15}{18}$ ____

6. $\frac{14}{30}$ ____

7. $\frac{11}{44}$ ____

8. $\frac{24}{36}$ ____

9. $\frac{12}{16}$ ____

10. $\frac{34}{68}$ ____

11. $\frac{28}{42}$ ____

12. $\frac{30}{65}$ ____

Write each fraction in simplest form. Give the GCF of the numerator and denominator.

13. $\frac{18}{45}$ ____ GCF = ____

14. $\frac{66}{121}$ ____ GCF = ____

15. $\frac{36}{102}$ ____ GCF = ____

16. $\frac{125}{200}$ ____ GCF = ____

17. $\frac{36}{64}$ ____ GCF = ____

18. $\frac{65}{90}$ ____ GCF = ____

19. $\frac{45}{72}$ ____ GCF = ____

20. $\frac{35}{85}$ ____ GCF = ____

21. $\frac{30}{42}$ ____ GCF = ____

Solve.

22. Emily exercised from 4:05 P.M. to 4:32 P.M. For what part of an hour did Emily exercise? Write the fraction in the simplest form. _____

23. Luis rode his bike after school for 48 min. For what part of an hour did he ride his bike? Write the fraction in the simplest form. _____

24. Philip played video games for 55 min before dinner. For what part of an hour did he play? _____

25. What part of an hour is your school lunch time? _____

26. Survey 12 people to find their favorite kind of pizza from the following choices. Write the results in fraction form. Then shade the pizza shape using different colors to indicate their choices.

Pizza Favorites
Cheese _____
Sausage _____
Pepperoni _____
Mushroom _____

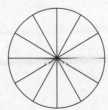

Course 2 Chapter 4

■■■■*Practice 4-7* *Problem-Solving Strategy:*
Look for a Pattern

Look for a pattern to solve each problem.

1. Find a pattern for the units digit of the powers of 7. What is the units digit of 7^{34}?

   _____

2. Find the sum of the two hundred even numbers from 0 to 398.

   _____

3. The figures at the right represent the first three *rectangular numbers*. Describe the pattern. Find the value of the eighth rectangular number.

   _____

   _____

4. The same cube is shown from three different angles. What color is on the bottom in the first position? (HINT: Cut out a model.)

   _____

   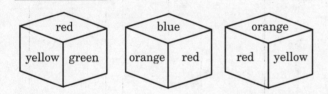

Use any strategy to solve each problem. Show all your work.

5. What is the greatest number of pieces of pizza you can form if you use five straight cuts across the pizza? _____

6. In this puzzle, each letter represents a digit. If a letter is used more than once, it represents the same digit each time. A true addition problem must result when you substitute digits for letters. (There is more than one answer possible.)

   $$\begin{array}{r} \text{S E V E N} \\ + \text{E I G H T} \\ \hline \text{T W E L V E} \end{array}$$

7. In a class of 34 students, 12 play the piano, 16 play football, and 12 play neither. How many play both piano and football?

   _____

8. What is the units digit of 6^6? _____

Practice 4-8 Mixed Numbers and Improper Fractions

1. Write a mixed number and an improper fraction for the model below. _____

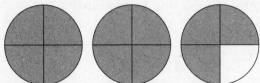

Write each mixed number as an improper fraction.

2. $2\frac{3}{8}$ _____

3. $5\frac{1}{3}$ _____

4. $1\frac{7}{10}$ _____

5. $3\frac{4}{9}$ _____

6. $4\frac{5}{8}$ _____

7. $3\frac{5}{12}$ _____

8. $1\frac{15}{16}$ _____

9. $2\frac{3}{10}$ _____

Write each improper fraction as a whole number or a mixed number in simplest form.

10. $\frac{25}{3}$ _____

11. $\frac{42}{7}$ _____

12. $\frac{18}{4}$ _____

13. $\frac{28}{6}$ _____

14. $\frac{27}{12}$ _____

15. $\frac{11}{6}$ _____

16. $\frac{20}{3}$ _____

17. $\frac{34}{8}$ _____

18. $\frac{125}{5}$ _____

19. $\frac{34}{7}$ _____

20. $\frac{40}{6}$ _____

21. $\frac{84}{12}$ _____

The distance around an indoor running track is $\frac{1}{16}$ mi.

22. Juan jogged around the track 40 times. How far did he jog? _____

23. Aaron walked around the track 36 times. How far did he walk?

_____

The distance around an outdoor running track is $\frac{1}{6}$ mile.

24. Aruna jogged around the track 16 times. How far did she jog?

_____

25. Theresa walked around the track 22 times. How far did she walk? _____

26. Shade the figures below to represent $3\frac{5}{8}$. How many eighths are shaded? _____

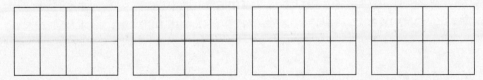

Practice 4-9 Fractions and Decimals

Choose a calculator, paper and pencil, or mental math to write each fraction as a decimal. Use a bar to indicate repeating digits.

1. $\frac{3}{5}$ _____   2. $\frac{7}{8}$ _____   3. $\frac{7}{9}$ _____   4. $\frac{5}{16}$ _____

5. $\frac{1}{6}$ _____   6. $\frac{5}{8}$ _____   7. $\frac{1}{3}$ _____   8. $\frac{2}{3}$ _____

9. $\frac{9}{10}$ _____   10. $\frac{7}{11}$ _____   11. $\frac{9}{20}$ _____   12. $\frac{3}{4}$ _____

13. $\frac{4}{9}$ _____   14. $\frac{9}{11}$ _____   15. $\frac{11}{20}$ _____   16. $\frac{9}{2}$ _____

17. $\frac{5}{4}$ _____   18. $\frac{11}{8}$ _____   19. $\frac{11}{12}$ _____   20. $\frac{8}{15}$ _____

Write each decimal as a fraction in simplest form.

21. 0.6 _____   22. 0.45 _____   23. 0.62 _____   24. 0.8 _____

25. 0.325 _____   26. 0.725 _____   27. 4.75 _____   28. 0.33 _____

29. 0.925 _____   30. 3.8 _____   31. 4.7 _____   32. 0.05 _____

33. 0.65 _____   34. 0.855 _____   35. 0.104 _____   36. 0.47 _____

37. 0.894 _____   38. 0.276 _____   39. 1.84 _____   40. 2.59 _____

Use the chart at the right for Exercises 41 and 42.

41. In which year did about $\frac{1}{10}$ of the families have four or more children?

    _____

42. In which year did about $\frac{1}{25}$ of the families have four or more children?

    _____

Year	Number of families (thousands)	Families with 4 or more children (thousands)
1970	51,586	5,055
1975	55,712	3,844
1980	59,550	2,441
1985	62,706	1,881
1990	66,090	1,851

Practice 5-1 Estimating with Fractions and Mixed Numbers

Estimate each sum or difference.

1. $\frac{1}{6} + \frac{5}{8}$ _____

2. $\frac{7}{8} - \frac{1}{16}$ _____

3. $\frac{9}{10} + \frac{7}{8}$ _____

4. $\frac{1}{12} + \frac{9}{10}$ _____

5. $\frac{1}{10} + \frac{5}{6}$ _____

6. $\frac{4}{5} - \frac{1}{6}$ _____

7. $\frac{11}{12} - \frac{5}{16}$ _____

8. $\frac{15}{16} + \frac{11}{12}$ _____

9. $2\frac{1}{6} + 7\frac{1}{9}$ _____

10. $4\frac{9}{10} - 3\frac{5}{8}$ _____

11. $4\frac{7}{8} + 8\frac{1}{5}$ _____

12. $14\frac{7}{9} - 9\frac{1}{8}$ _____

13. $14\frac{3}{4} + 9\frac{7}{8}$ _____

14. $7\frac{11}{15} - 6\frac{7}{16}$ _____

15. $3\frac{11}{15} - 2\frac{9}{10}$ _____

16. $8\frac{7}{8} - \frac{11}{12}$ _____

Estimate each product or quotient.

17. $13\frac{1}{8} \div 6\frac{1}{5}$ _____

18. $5\frac{1}{6} \cdot 8\frac{4}{5}$ _____

19. $8\frac{1}{6} \div 1\frac{9}{10}$ _____

20. $1\frac{9}{10} \cdot 4\frac{7}{8}$ _____

21. $27\frac{6}{7} \div 3\frac{2}{3}$ _____

22. $20\frac{4}{5} \cdot 2\frac{2}{7}$ _____

23. $9\frac{1}{3} \div 2\frac{7}{8}$ _____

24. $16\frac{1}{9} \cdot 2\frac{1}{8}$ _____

25. $19\frac{4}{5} \div 4\frac{5}{8}$ _____

26. $9\frac{2}{13} \div 3\frac{1}{18}$ _____

27. $42\frac{1}{6} \div 6\frac{1}{16}$ _____

28. $3\frac{9}{10} \cdot 8\frac{7}{8}$ _____

29. $15\frac{1}{20} \cdot 3\frac{1}{10}$ _____

30. $72\frac{2}{15} \div 8\frac{3}{4}$ _____

31. $3\frac{5}{6} \cdot 10\frac{1}{12}$ _____

32. $36\frac{1}{4} \div 5\frac{15}{16}$ _____

Solve each problem.

33. Each dress for a wedding party requires $7\frac{1}{8}$ yd of material. Estimate the amount of material you would need to make 6 dresses.

_____

34. A fabric store has $80\frac{3}{8}$ yd of a particular fabric. About how many pairs of curtains could be made from this fabric if each pair requires $4\frac{1}{8}$ yd of fabric?

_____

35. Adam's car can hold $16\frac{1}{10}$ gal of gasoline. About how many gallons are left if he started with a full tank and has used $11\frac{9}{10}$ gal?

_____

36. Julia bought stock at $\$28\frac{1}{8}$ per share. The value of each stock increased by $\$6\frac{5}{8}$. About how much is each share of stock now worth?

_____

Practice 5-2 Adding and Subtracting Fractions

Write a number sentence for each model shown.

1.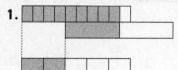

2.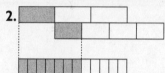

3.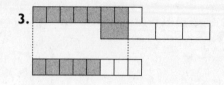

_____   _____   _____

Find each sum or difference.

4. $\frac{1}{6} + \frac{7}{8}$ ____

5. $\frac{9}{10} - \frac{1}{6}$ ____

6. $\frac{4}{5} + \frac{9}{10}$ ____

7. $\frac{1}{6} + \frac{1}{6}$ ____

8. $\frac{1}{10} + \frac{2}{5}$ ____

9. $\frac{8}{9} - \frac{2}{9}$ ____

10. $\frac{5}{6} + \frac{1}{12}$ ____

11. $\frac{2}{3} - \frac{1}{2}$ ____

12. $\frac{3}{10} + \frac{3}{10}$ ____

13. $\frac{7}{9} - \frac{1}{3}$ ____

14. $\frac{3}{4} - \frac{1}{4}$ ____

15. $\frac{3}{8} + \frac{5}{12}$ ____

16. $\frac{1}{5} + \frac{3}{4}$ ____

17. $\frac{1}{3} + \frac{1}{2}$ ____

18. $\frac{11}{12} - \frac{3}{4}$ ____

19. $\frac{1}{8} + \frac{1}{12}$ ____

20. $\frac{7}{10} - \frac{1}{3}$ ____

21. $\frac{5}{8} + \frac{1}{4}$ ____

Use the table at the right for Exercises 22–27. Tell which two snacks combine to make each amount.

22. $\frac{5}{6}$ c _____

23. $\frac{1}{2}$ c _____

24. $\frac{3}{4}$ c _____

25. $\frac{11}{12}$ c _____

26. 1 c _____

27. $\frac{19}{24}$ c _____

Snack	Serving Amount
Raisins	$\frac{1}{4}$ c
Peanuts	$\frac{3}{8}$ c
Chocolate chips	$\frac{1}{8}$ c
Sesame sticks	$\frac{2}{3}$ c
Mini pretzels	$\frac{5}{8}$ c
Dried apricots	$\frac{1}{6}$ c

Practice 5-3 *Adding and Subtracting Mixed Numbers*

Find each sum.

1. $5\frac{1}{3} + 3\frac{2}{3}$ _____

2. $7\frac{1}{4} + 4\frac{3}{8}$ _____

3. $2\frac{1}{8} + 6\frac{5}{8}$ _____

4. $8\frac{1}{5} + 4\frac{3}{10}$ _____

5. $9\frac{1}{6} + 6\frac{1}{4}$ _____

6. $3\frac{2}{3} + 10\frac{5}{6}$ _____

Find each difference.

7. $6\frac{11}{12} - 4\frac{5}{12}$ _____

8. $12 - 5\frac{3}{10}$ _____

9. $14\frac{1}{2} - 7\frac{1}{5}$ _____

10. $9 - 5\frac{5}{6}$ _____

11. $13\frac{3}{4} - 10\frac{1}{2}$ _____

12. $15\frac{1}{6} - 6\frac{5}{12}$ _____

Find each sum or difference.

13. $1\frac{1}{6} - \frac{3}{4}$ _____

14. $4\frac{1}{2} - 2\frac{7}{8}$ _____

15. $9\frac{3}{4} + 7\frac{7}{8}$ _____

16. $5\frac{1}{6} - 4\frac{7}{12}$ _____

17. $9\frac{8}{15} + 11\frac{5}{12}$ _____

18. $\frac{14}{15} - \frac{1}{2}$ _____

19. $\frac{7}{12} + \frac{5}{6}$ _____

20. $1\frac{4}{9} + 3\frac{1}{6}$ _____

21. $3\frac{1}{2} - 2\frac{1}{4}$ _____

Circle A, B, C, or D. Which of the following represents each period of time as a fraction in lowest terms?

22. 8:00 A.M. to 9:20 A.M.

   A. $1\frac{1}{3}$ h   **B.** $1\frac{1}{2}$ h

   C. $\frac{1}{3}$ h   **D.** $1\frac{2}{3}$ h

23. 9:00 A.M. to 2:45 P.M.

   A. $5\frac{2}{3}$ h   **B.** $7\frac{3}{4}$ h

   C. $4\frac{3}{4}$ h   **D.** $5\frac{3}{4}$ h

24. 11:00 A.M. to 3:55 P.M.

   A. $3\frac{11}{12}$ h   **B.** $4\frac{11}{12}$ h

   C. $4\frac{55}{60}$ h   **D.** $4\frac{11}{10}$ h

25. 8:30 A.M. to 10:40 P.M.

   A. $2\frac{1}{6}$ h   **B.** $2\frac{1}{5}$ h

   C. $14\frac{1}{6}$ h   **D.** $14\frac{2}{3}$ h

26. 5:30 P.M. to 10:45 P.M.

   A. $4\frac{3}{4}$ h   **B.** $5\frac{1}{4}$ h

   C. $6\frac{1}{6}$ h   **D.** $5\frac{1}{5}$ h

27. 7:20 A.M. to 11:00 A.M.

   A. $3\frac{2}{3}$ h   **B.** $3\frac{1}{15}$ h

   C. $2\frac{1}{3}$ h   **D.** $4\frac{1}{4}$ h

▬ Practice 5-4 Solving Equations with Fractions by Adding and Subtracting

Write and solve the equation represented by each model.

1.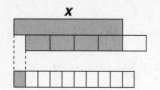
   _____

2.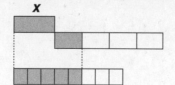
   _____

3.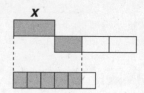
   _____

Solve each equation.

4. $m + \frac{7}{8} = 1\frac{1}{2}$ _____

5. $j - \frac{1}{4} = \frac{7}{8}$ _____

6. $t + \frac{9}{10} = 1\frac{4}{5}$ _____

7. $k - \frac{5}{6} = \frac{11}{12}$ _____

8. $\frac{7}{8} = n + \frac{1}{4}$ _____

9. $\frac{1}{5} = a - \frac{9}{10}$ _____

10. $b + \frac{7}{10} = 1\frac{1}{2}$ _____

11. $c - \frac{7}{8} = \frac{5}{8}$ _____

12. $w + 2\frac{1}{4} = 5\frac{5}{8}$ _____

13. $x - 1\frac{3}{5} = 2\frac{7}{10}$ _____

14. $\frac{2}{9} = z - \frac{2}{3}$ _____

15. $\frac{1}{2} = d + \frac{1}{6}$ _____

16. $4\frac{3}{4} + q = 5\frac{7}{8}$ _____

17. $9\frac{1}{4} = h - 1\frac{3}{4}$ _____

18. $e + 6\frac{3}{4} = 9\frac{7}{8}$ _____

19. $f - 5\frac{1}{2} = 8\frac{2}{3}$ _____

20. $u + 7\frac{1}{6} = 9\frac{5}{12}$ _____

21. $e - 4\frac{1}{6} = 7\frac{5}{6}$ _____

22. $i + 7\frac{1}{3} = 9\frac{11}{12}$ _____

23. $k - 8\frac{1}{5} = 7\frac{2}{5}$ _____

24. $p + 4\frac{2}{9} = 11\frac{1}{3}$ _____

Solve each problem by writing and solving an equation.

25. Lacey had a ribbon $5\frac{7}{8}$ yd long. She used $1\frac{1}{2}$ yd for a belt for a dress. What length of the ribbon remains?

    _____

26. The depth of a river at one spot is normally $16\frac{3}{4}$ ft deep. The water rose $5\frac{1}{2}$ ft during a flood. What was the depth of the river at that spot during the flood?

    _____

27. Katrina rode her bicycle $6\frac{3}{4}$ mi before she realized she forgot her lock. She rode $2\frac{1}{2}$ mi toward home before she met Magda. How far does Katrina need to ride before she is home?

    _____

28. A shoreline is washing away at a rate of $1\frac{7}{10}$ ft each year. A house is $225\frac{9}{10}$ ft from the water. If erosion continues at the same rate, how far from the water will the house be next year?

    _____

Practice 5-5 Multiplying Fractions and Mixed Numbers

Write a multiplication sentence for each model. Write the product as a fraction in simplest form.

1.

2.

3.

_____   _____   _____

Find each product.

4. $\frac{5}{6} \cdot \frac{3}{5}$ _____

5. $\frac{7}{8} \cdot \frac{4}{5}$ _____

6. $\frac{9}{10} \cdot \frac{5}{12}$ _____

7. $\frac{5}{8} \cdot \frac{3}{5}$ _____

8. $\frac{1}{6}$ of 36 _____

9. $\frac{2}{3}$ of 36 _____

10. $\frac{5}{9} \cdot 36$ _____

11. $\frac{3}{4} \cdot 36$ _____

12. $5 \cdot \frac{3}{4}$ _____

13. $2 \cdot \frac{9}{10}$ _____

14. $8 \cdot \frac{9}{10}$ _____

15. $4 \cdot \frac{7}{12}$ _____

16. $\frac{1}{4} \cdot 3\frac{1}{3}$ _____

17. $\frac{5}{6}$ of $1\frac{3}{5}$ _____

18. $\frac{4}{5} \cdot 2\frac{5}{6}$ _____

19. $\frac{1}{8}$ of $1\frac{4}{5}$ _____

20. $3 \cdot 4\frac{1}{2}$ _____

21. $4 \cdot 2\frac{2}{3}$ _____

22. $5 \cdot 2\frac{1}{4}$ _____

23. $3 \cdot 2\frac{2}{3}$ _____

24. $4\frac{1}{2} \cdot 1\frac{1}{6}$ _____

25. $3\frac{2}{3} \cdot 1\frac{1}{2}$ _____

26. $4\frac{1}{6} \cdot 2\frac{2}{5}$ _____

27. $3\frac{1}{4} \cdot 2\frac{1}{6}$ _____

Find the area of each rectangle.

28.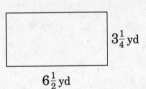

$3\frac{1}{4}$ yd

$6\frac{1}{2}$ yd

29.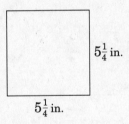

$5\frac{1}{4}$ in.

$5\frac{1}{4}$ in.

_____   _____

30.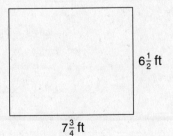

$6\frac{1}{2}$ ft

$7\frac{3}{4}$ ft

31.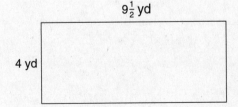

$9\frac{1}{2}$ yd

4 yd

_____   _____

▰▰▰ *Practice 5-6* Dividing Fractions and Mixed Numbers

Find the reciprocal of each number.

1. $\frac{1}{2}$ ____   2. $\frac{3}{4}$ ____   3. $\frac{7}{8}$ ____   4. $\frac{9}{16}$ ____   5. $\frac{4}{5}$ ____

6. $1\frac{1}{4}$ ____   7. $2\frac{1}{3}$ ____   8. $3\frac{2}{5}$ ____   9. $2\frac{9}{10}$ ____   10. $3\frac{1}{6}$ ____

Choose a calculator, paper and pencil, or mental math to find each quotient.

11. $\frac{3}{4} \div \frac{1}{4}$ ____   12. $\frac{7}{8} \div \frac{1}{4}$ ____   13. $\frac{5}{6} \div \frac{1}{12}$ ____   14. $\frac{1}{12} \div \frac{5}{6}$ ____

15. $4 \div \frac{1}{3}$ ____   16. $6 \div \frac{3}{4}$ ____   17. $5 \div \frac{9}{10}$ ____   18. $8 \div \frac{2}{3}$ ____

19. $\frac{4}{5} \div 2$ ____   20. $\frac{7}{8} \div 3$ ____   21. $\frac{5}{6} \div 5$ ____   22. $\frac{4}{9} \div 8$ ____

23. $1\frac{1}{2} \div \frac{2}{3}$ ____   24. $1\frac{1}{2} \div \frac{3}{2}$ ____   25. $\frac{3}{4} \div 1\frac{1}{3}$ ____   26. $2\frac{1}{2} \div 1\frac{1}{4}$ ____

27. $2\frac{1}{2} \div 2\frac{1}{4}$ ____   28. $1\frac{3}{4} \div \frac{3}{4}$ ____   29. $1\frac{7}{10} \div \frac{1}{2}$ ____   30. $3\frac{1}{4} \div 1\frac{1}{3}$ ____

31. $4\frac{1}{2} \div 2\frac{1}{2}$ ____   32. $6 \div 3\frac{4}{5}$ ____   33. $4\frac{3}{4} \div \frac{7}{8}$ ____   34. $5\frac{5}{6} \div 1\frac{1}{3}$ ____

35. $3\frac{3}{8} \div 1\frac{1}{4}$ ____   36. $6\frac{1}{2} \div 1\frac{1}{2}$ ____   37. $2\frac{9}{10} \div 1\frac{3}{4}$ ____   38. $7\frac{5}{8} \div 4\frac{1}{2}$ ____

Solve each problem.

39. Rosa makes $2\frac{1}{2}$ c of pudding. How many $\frac{1}{3}$ c servings can she get from the pudding?

40. One type of lightning bug glows once every $1\frac{1}{2}$ s. How many times can it glow in 1 min?

_____

_____

41. Bea can run $\frac{1}{6}$ mi in 2 min. How long should it take her to run 2 mi?

42. Joe drives 20 mi in $\frac{1}{2}$ h. How long will it take him to drive 50 mi?

_____

_____

■■■ *Practice 5-7* Problem-Solving Strategy: Work Backward

Work backward to solve each problem.

1. A fast-growing mushroom doubled in size every day. After 30 days, it measured 6 in. tall. On which day did it measure $1\frac{1}{2}$ in. tall? _____

2. If you start with a number, subtract 14, then divide by 12, the result is 248. What was the original number? _____

3. Mrs. Wainright is in a car pool. It takes her 20 min to pick up her passengers. From her last stop, it takes her 45 min to drive to the office. The group likes to arrive 10 min before office hours begin. If office hours start at 8:30 A.M., what time should Mrs. Wainright leave her apartment?

_____

Use any strategy to solve each problem. Show your work.

4. James went shopping one Saturday afternoon. He spent $\frac{1}{2}$ of the money he had on a new stereo system. He spent half of the money he had left on a new suit. Half of what remained, he spent on a new sweater. Half of what remained, he spent on a new CD. If he went home with $15, how much money did he have to begin with? _____

5. At a middle school, half the students leave immediately after school because they walk home. After 5 min, $\frac{1}{4}$ of the students remaining are gone, riding home on their bicycles. After another 5 min, $\frac{3}{4}$ of those remaining depart on buses. At this time, 51 students remain for after-school activities. How many students attend the middle school?

_____

6. Trish spent a fourth of her money on a new book. She paid a friend $3.50 that she had borrowed. Later she spent $4.75 on a pair of earrings. When she arrived home, she had $18.00. How much money did she have to start with? _____

7. During one day, Howard wrote checks for $125.00, $98.57, and $23.46. He made a deposit of $475.00. If his account now has $472.96, how much was in the account at the start of the day? _____

8. If you start with a number, add $\frac{2}{5}$, then multiply by 7, the result is $6\frac{3}{10}$. What was the original number?

_____

Practice 5-8 Changing Units in the Customary System

Tell whether you would multiply or divide to change from one unit of measure to the other.

1. tons to pounds

_____

2. pints to quarts

_____

3. feet to yards

_____

4. gallons to pints

_____

5. cups to quarts

_____

6. pounds to ounces

_____

Choose a calculator, paper and pencil, or mental math to change from one unit of measure to the other.

7. 9 qt = _____ gal

8. $2\frac{1}{4}$ T = _____ lb

9. $3\frac{1}{2}$ yd = _____ in.

10. 4 yd = _____ ft

11. 60 c = _____ qt

12. $1\frac{3}{4}$ gal = _____ pt

13. 246 in. = _____ ft

14. 1,750 oz = _____ lb

15. $\frac{3}{4}$ T = _____ oz

16. 84 ft = _____ yd

17. 198 in. = _____ yd

18. 11,880 ft = _____ mi

19. 480 fl oz = _____ pt

20. $\frac{1}{4}$ gal = _____ fl oz

21. $1\frac{1}{2}$ pt = _____ fl oz

22. $\frac{1}{2}$ mi = _____ ft

23. $\frac{1}{10}$ mi = _____ in.

24. 3 mi = _____ yd

25. 2 lb 6 oz = _____ lb

26. 2 qt 8 fl oz = _____ qt

27. 4 yd 2 ft = _____ yd

Find the perimeter of each rectangle in feet and in inches.

28. $6\frac{1}{2}$ ft

$2\frac{1}{4}$ ft

_____

29.   6 ft 3 in.

5 ft 2 in.

_____

30.   426 in.

352 in.

_____

Practice 5-9 Solving Equations with Fractions by Mutliplying and Dividing

Choose a calculator, paper and pencil, or mental math to solve each equation.

1. $4y = 9$ _____

2. $\frac{d}{9} = 16$ _____

3. $\frac{1}{5}a = 47$ _____

4. $51m = 3$ _____

5. $\frac{x}{9} = 4$ _____

6. $5j = 50$ _____

7. $16b = 2$ _____

8. $\frac{1}{4}c = 9$ _____

9. $\frac{z}{12} = 8$ _____

10. $11e = 15$ _____

11. $50p = 75$ _____

12. $19 = \frac{1}{6}q$ _____

13. $\frac{k}{29} = 71$ _____

14. $15v = 34$ _____

15. $\frac{1}{16}t = 24$ _____

16. $96 = 8v$ _____

17. $\frac{x}{19} = 56$ _____

18. $8f = 12$ _____

19. $\frac{g}{58} = 29$ _____

20. $26i = 50$ _____

21. $\frac{k}{12} = 144$ _____

22. $18m = 30$ _____

23. $\frac{1}{20}n = 75$ _____

24. $\frac{r}{25} = 100$ _____

25. $\frac{1}{6}s = 12$ _____

26. $21u = 42$ _____

27. $\frac{x}{18} = 36$ _____

28. $\frac{y}{15} = 27$ _____

29. $15z = 27$ _____

30. $\frac{1}{9}a = 51$ _____

Solve.

31. If $\frac{1}{3}$ of a number is 21, what is the number?

_____

32. If 8 times a number is 15, what is the number?

_____

33. On a certain day, 240 cars along a certain stretch of highway had two or more people in them. If this was $\frac{2}{5}$ of the cars along that stretch of road, how many cars were there? _____

34. In a store, $\frac{1}{6}$ of the slacks on a rack were black. If there were 8 pairs of black slacks, how many pairs of slacks were on that rack?

_____

Practice 6-1 Exploring Ratios Using Data

Write a ratio in three ways for each situation.

1. Ten years ago in Louisiana, in 1988, schools averaged 182 pupils for every 10 teachers.

   _____

2. In a recent year, 41 out of 250 people in the labor force belonged to a union.

   _____

3. Between 1899–1900, 284 out of 1,000 people in the United States were 5–17 years old.

   _____

4. In a recent year, 7 out of 10 people with Japanese heritage who lived in the United States lived in either Hawaii or California.

   _____

Use the chart below for Exercises 5–6.

The seventh-grade classes were asked whether they wanted chicken or pasta served at their awards banquet.

Room Number	Chicken	Pasta
201	10	12
202	8	17
203	16	10

5. In room 201, what is the ratio of students who prefer chicken to students who prefer pasta?

   _____

6. Combine the totals for all three rooms. What is the ratio of the number of students who prefer pasta to the number of students who prefer chicken?

   _____

Write each ratio in simplest form.

7. $\frac{2}{6}$ _____

8. $3:21$ _____

9. 16 to 20 _____

10. $\frac{3}{30}$ _____

11. 12 to 18 _____

12. $81:27$ _____

13. $\frac{6}{28}$ _____

14. 49 to 14 _____

Choose A, B, C, or D.

15. A bag contains green, yellow, and orange marbles. The ratio of green marbles to yellow marbles is 2 : 5. The ratio of yellow marbles to orange marbles is 3 : 4. What is the ratio of green marbles to orange marbles? _____

   A. 5 : 2   **B.** 15 : 8   **C.** 5 : 4   **D.** 3 : 10

Practice 6-2 Unit Rates and Proportional Reasoning

Write the unit rate for each situation.

1. travel 250 mi in 5 h

   _____

2. earn $75.20 in 8 h

   _____

3. read 80 pages in 2 h

   _____

4. type 8,580 words in 2 h 45 min

   _____

5. manufacture 2,488 parts in 8 h

   _____

6. 50 copies of a book on 2 shelves

   _____

7. $30 for 6 books

   _____

8. 24 points in 3 games

   _____

Find each unit price. Then determine the better buy.

9. paper: 100 sheets for $.99
   500 sheets for $4.29

   _____

10. peanuts: 1 lb for $1.29
    12 oz for $.95

    _____

11. crackers: 15 oz for $1.79
    12 oz for $1.49

    _____

12. apples: 3 lb for $1.89
    5 lb for $2.49

    _____

13. mechanical pencils: 4 for $1.25
    25 for $5.69

    _____

14. bagels: 4 for $.89
    6 for $1.39

    _____

15. orange juice: 12 oz for $1.49
    16 oz for $1.89

    _____

16. socks: 3 pairs for $4.29
    8 pairs for $10.79

    _____

17. **a.** Yolanda and Yoko ran in a 100-yd dash. When Yolanda
    crossed the finish line, Yoko was 10 yd behind her. The girls
    then repeated the race, with Yolanda starting 10 yd behind
    the starting line. If each girl ran at the same rate as before,
    who won the race? By how many yards?

    _____

   b. Assuming the girls run at the same rate as before, how far
    behind the starting line should Yolanda be in order for the
    two to finish in a tie?

    _____

■■■ Practice 6-3 Proportions

Choose a calculator, paper and pencil, or mental math.
Which pairs of ratios form a proportion?

1. $\frac{12}{16}, \frac{30}{40}$ _____

2. $\frac{8}{12}, \frac{15}{21}$ _____

3. $\frac{27}{21}, \frac{81}{56}$ _____

4. $\frac{45}{24}, \frac{75}{40}$ _____

5. $\frac{5}{9}, \frac{80}{117}$ _____

6. $\frac{15}{25}, \frac{75}{125}$ _____

Choose a calculator, paper and pencil, or mental math. Find the value of *n* in each proportion.

7. $\frac{n}{14} = \frac{20}{35}$ _____

8. $\frac{9}{6} = \frac{21}{n}$ _____

9. $\frac{24}{n} = \frac{16}{10}$ _____

10. $\frac{3}{4} = \frac{n}{10}$ _____

11. $\frac{n}{4} = \frac{17}{3}$ _____

12. $\frac{25}{n} = \frac{9}{8}$ _____

Choose A, B, or C.

13. A contractor estimates it will cost \$2,400 to build a deck to a customer's specifications. Which proportion would help you find how much it would cost to build five similar decks? _____

    A. $\frac{1}{5} = \frac{n}{\$2,400}$ **B.** $\frac{1}{\$2,400} = \frac{n}{5}$ **C.** $\frac{1}{\$2,400} = \frac{5}{n}$

14. A recipe requires 3 c of flour to make 27 dinner rolls. Which of the proportions would help you find the flour needed to make 9 rolls? _____

    A. $\frac{3}{9} = \frac{n}{27}$ **B.** $\frac{3}{27} = \frac{9}{n}$ **C.** $\frac{27}{3} = \frac{9}{n}$

Choose a calculator, paper and pencil, or mental math.

15. Mandy runs 4 km in 18 min. She plans to run in a 15 km race. How long will it take her to complete the race?

    _____

16. Ken's new car can go 26 mi/gal of gas. The car's gasoline tank holds 14 gal. How far will he be able to go on a full tank?

    _____

17. Eleanor can complete two skirts in 15 days. How long will it take her to complete eight skirts?

    _____

18. Three eggs are required to make two dozen muffins. How many eggs are needed to make 12 dozen muffins?

    _____

■ **Practice 6-4** *Using Similar Figures*

$\triangle MNO \sim \triangle JKL$. **Find each of the corresponding parts.**

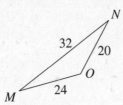

1. $\angle M$ corresponds to _____.

2. $\angle L$ corresponds to _____.

3. $\overline{ON}$ corresponds to _____.

4. $\angle K$ corresponds to _____.

5. $\overline{JL}$ corresponds to _____.

6. $\overline{MN}$ corresponds to _____.

7. What is the ratio of the lengths of the corresponding sides? _____

Choose a calculator, paper and pencil, or mental math. The pairs of figures below are similar. Use proportions to find the values of x and y.

8.
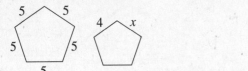
_____

9.
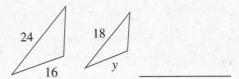
_____

10.
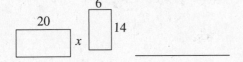
_____

11.
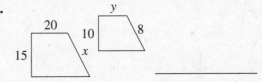
_____

12.
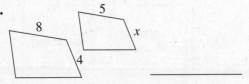
_____

13.
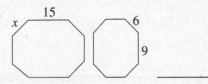
_____

Draw lines to show how to divide the figure at the right into 12 pieces as described in Exercises 14 and 15. Each new piece must have the same size and shape as the other new pieces.

14. The shapes should be rectangles.

15. The shapes should be triangles.

▰▰▰ *Practice 6-5* *Exploring Maps and Scale Drawings*

The scale of a map is 2 cm : 21 km. Find the actual distances for the following map distances.

1. 9 cm _____

2. 12.5 cm _____

3. 14 mm _____

4. 3.6 m _____

5. 4.5 cm _____

6. 7.1 cm _____

7. 7.18 cm _____

8. 25 cm _____

9. 1 cm _____

A scale drawing has a scale of $\frac{1}{4}$ in. : 12 ft. Find the length on the drawing for each actual length.

10. 8 ft _____

11. 30 ft _____

12. 15 ft _____

13. 56 ft _____

14. 18 ft _____

15. 20 ft _____

16. 40 ft _____

17. 80 ft _____

Use a metric ruler to find the approximate distance between the towns.

18. Hitchcockburg to Kidville _____

19. Dodgetown to Earp City _____

20. Dodgetown to Kidville _____

21. Kidville to Earp City _____

22. Dodgetown to Hitchcockburg _____

23. Earp City to Hitchcockburg _____

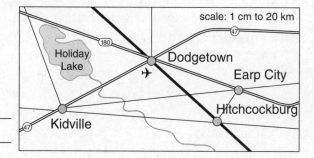

Solve.

24. The scale drawing shows a two-bedroom apartment. The master bedroom is 9 ft × 12 ft. Use an inch ruler to measure the drawing.

    a. The scale is _____

    b. Write the actual dimensions in place of the scale dimensions.

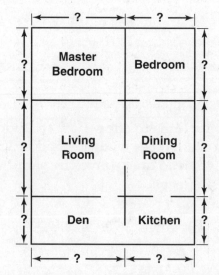

Practice 6-6 Modeling Percents

Shade each grid to represent each of the following percents.

1. 53%

2. 123%

3. 71%

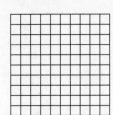
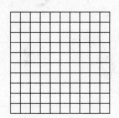
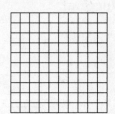

Rewrite each ratio as a percent.

4. $\frac{4}{5}$ _____

5. $\frac{3}{5}$ _____

6. $\frac{9}{10}$ _____

7. $\frac{3}{10}$ _____

8. $\frac{6}{25}$ _____

9. $\frac{7}{100}$ _____

10. $\frac{9}{50}$ _____

11. $\frac{9}{25}$ _____

12. $\frac{2}{5}$ _____

13. $\frac{7}{10}$ _____

14. $\frac{4}{25}$ _____

15. $\frac{16}{25}$ _____

16. $\frac{11}{20}$ _____

17. $\frac{19}{20}$ _____

18. $\frac{27}{50}$ _____

19. 41 : 50 _____

Write the percent of each figure that is shaded.

20.

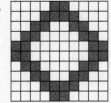

_____

21.

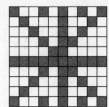

_____

22.

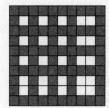

_____

Complete the following.

Ancient Egyptians did not write the fraction $\frac{4}{5}$ as "$\frac{4}{5}$". Instead, they used unit fractions. The numerator of a unit fraction is always 1. No denominator used to represent a given fraction can be repeated. For this reason, Egyptians would have written $\frac{4}{5}$ as $\frac{1}{2} + \frac{1}{5} + \frac{1}{10}$ and not as $\frac{1}{2} + \frac{1}{10} + \frac{1}{10} + \frac{1}{10}$. Write each of the following as a sum of unit fractions.

23. $\frac{3}{4}$ _____

24. $\frac{5}{8}$ _____

25. $\frac{9}{10}$ _____

26. $\frac{7}{12}$ _____

27. $\frac{11}{12}$ _____

28. $\frac{11}{15}$ _____

Practice 6-7 Percents, Fractions, and Decimals

**Choose a calculator, paper and pencil, or mental math.
Write each percent as a fraction in simplest form and as a
decimal.**

1. 65% _____ **2.** 37.5% _____ **3.** 80% _____ **4.** 25% _____

5. 18% _____ **6.** 46% _____ **7.** 87% _____ **8.** 8% _____

9. 43% _____ **10.** 55% _____ **11.** 94% _____ **12.** 36% _____

**Write each number as a percent. Round to the nearest tenth
of a percent where necessary.**

13. $\frac{7}{10}$ _____ **14.** 0.635 _____ **15.** 3.7 _____ **16.** $\frac{8}{15}$ _____

17. $\frac{7}{50}$ _____ **18.** 0.56 _____ **19.** 4.13 _____ **20.** $\frac{3}{8}$ _____

21. $\frac{7}{12}$ _____ **22.** 0.387 _____ **23.** 2.83 _____ **24.** $\frac{2}{9}$ _____

**Write each number as a percent. Place the number into the
puzzle without using the percent sign or decimal point.**

Across

1. 1.34

3. $\frac{53}{100}$

5. $5\frac{13}{20}$

7. $\frac{228}{200}$

9. 0.0456

10. 0.63

11. $\frac{11}{2,000}$

13. 0.58

14. 0.00905

16. 0.605

Down

2. 3.46

4. 0.324

5. $\frac{1}{2}$

6. 0.515

8. $\frac{33}{200}$

9. 43.8

10. $\frac{659}{1,000}$

12. 5.435

15. $\frac{14}{25}$

Practice 6-8 Problem-Solving Strategy: Use Multiple Strategies

Choose any strategy to solve. Show all your work.

1. Find four consecutive numbers that have a sum of 118.

   _____

2. Use the digits 3, 6, 7, and 8. Find all of the four-digit numbers that are divisible by 6. Use a digit only once in each number.

   _____

   _____

3. A baby was 20 in. long at birth. The baby's body was 10 in. longer than the length of her head. How long was her head?

   _____

4. Frank and Ernest live 220 mi apart. They decide to meet at noon one Saturday at a restaurant exactly halfway between them. Frank will drive at a constant speed of 55 mi/h. Ernest will only drive at a constant speed of 50 mi/h. In order to meet at noon, when should each person leave home?

   _____

5. Find three consecutive numbers that have a sum of 381.

   _____

6. Use the digits 1, 2, 7, and 8. Find all of the four-digit numbers that are divisible by 4. Use a digit only once in each number.

   _____

7. Samuel had a board 5 ft long that he cut into two pieces. One piece was 8 in. longer than the other. How long was the shorter board?

   _____

8. A fenced-in yard has length of 80 ft and width of 120 ft. The fence has a post every 4 ft. How many posts are there?

   _____

Practice 6-9 *Finding the Percent of a Number*

Find each answer.

1. What is 20% of 560?

2. What is 42% of 200?

3. What is 9% of 50?

_____

_____

_____

4. Find 40% of 70.

5. What is 25% of 80?

6. What is 50% of 80?

_____

_____

_____

7. What is 40% of 200?

8. Find 5% of 80.

9. What is 75% of 200?

_____

_____

_____

Choose a calculator, paper and pencil, or mental math to solve.

10. What is 14% of 120?

11. Find 30% of 180.

12. What is 62.5% of 24?

_____

_____

_____

13. What is 34% of 50?

14. What is 25% of 240?

15. Find 85.5% of 23.

_____

_____

_____

16. What is 120% of 56?

17. Find 80% of 90.

18. What is 42% of 120?

_____

_____

_____

Farmer Jones raised a watermelon that weighed 20 lb. From his experience with raising watermelons, he estimated that 95% of the watermelon's weight is water.

19. How much of the watermelon is water? _____

20. How much of the watermelon is not water? _____

21. The watermelon was shipped off to market. There it sat, until it had dehydrated (lost water) and only 90% of the watermelon's weight was water. If the watermelon is now only 90% water, what percent of it is not water? _____

22. The solid part of the watermelon still weighs the same. What was the weight of the watermelon at this point?

_____

Solve.

23. A bicycle goes on sale at 75% of its original price of $160. What is its sale price?

_____

■■■■Practice 6-10 *Using Proportions with Percents*

Write a proportion and solve.

1. 48 is 60% of what
   number? _____

2. What is 175% of 85?
   _____

3. What percent of 90 is 50?
   _____

4. 76 is 80% of what
   number? _____

5. What is 50% of 42.88?
   _____

6. 96 is 160% of what
   number? _____

7. What percent of 24
   is 72? _____

8. What is 85% of 120?
   _____

9. What is 80% of 12?
   _____

10. 56 is 75% of what
    number? _____

11. What percent of 80
    is 50? _____

12. 85 is what percent of
    200? _____

Choose a calculator, paper and pencil, or mental math to solve.

13. The sale price of a bicycle is $120. This is 75% of the original
    price. Find the original price.

    _____

14. The attendance at the Brown family reunion was 160 people.
    This was 125% of last year's attendance. How many people
    attended the reunion last year?

    _____

15. A company has 875 employees. On "Half-Price Wednesday," 64%
    of the employees eat lunch at the company cafeteria. How many
    employees eat lunch at the cafeteria on Wednesdays?

    _____

16. There are 1,295 students attending a small university. There
    are 714 women enrolled. What percentage of students are
    women?

    _____

▬▬▬*Practice 6-11* Finding Percent of Change

Find the percent of change. State whether each change is an increase or a decrease.

1. A $50 coat is put on sale for $35.

_____

2. Mayelle earns $18,000 a year. After a raise, she earns $19,500.

_____

3. Last year Anthony earned $24,000. After a brief lay-off this year, Anthony's income is $18,500.

_____

4. In 1981, about $1.1 million was lost due to fires. In 1988, the loss was about $9.6 million.

_____

5. In a recent year, certain colleges and universities received about $268 million in aid. Ten years later, they received about $94 million.

_____

6. A coat regularly costing $125 is put on sale for $75.

_____

7. Suppose that at a job interview, you are told that you would receive a 10% increase in your salary at the end of each of the first three years. How much would your starting salary have changed at the end of the third year?

_____

8. Four years ago there were 35 students in the school band. Since then 12 students have joined the band.

_____

9. Complete the table.

Enrollment in Center City Schools From 1990 to 1995

Year	Enrollment	Change from Last Year (Number of Students)	Change from Last Year (%)	Increase or Decrease
1990	18,500	—	—	—
1991	19,300			
1992	19,700			
1993	19,500			
1994	19,870			
1995	19,200			

Practice 7-1 Exploring Visual Patterns

1. Draw the next two figures for the pattern shown below.

_____

2. Describe the twentieth figure for the pattern in Exercise 1.

_____

Draw the next two figures for each pattern.

3.

_____

4.

_____

Circle A, B, C, or D. Choose the figure that continues each pattern.

5.

A.   B.   C.   D.

6.

A.   B.   C.   D.

7.

A.   B.   C.   D.

Practice 7-2 Classifying and Measuring Angles

Estimate the measure of each angle. Then classify the angle.

1.   2.   3.

_____   _____   _____

Classify each angle as *acute, right, obtuse,* or *straight.*

4. $m\angle A = 180°$ 5. $m\angle B = 43°$ 6. $m\angle C = 127°$ 7. $m\angle D = 90°$

_____   _____   _____   _____

Use the diagram at the right. Name each of the following.

8. four lines   _____

9. three segments   _____

10. four rays   _____

11. four right angles   12. two pairs of obtuse vertical angles

_____   _____

13. two pairs of adjacent supplementary   14. two pairs of complementary angles
    angles
_____
_____

15. Use a protractor to find $m\angle A$, $m\angle B$, $m\angle C$, and $m\angle D$.

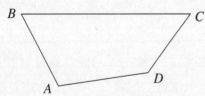

_____

_____

_____

_____

16. Use a protractor. Draw two vertical   17. Use the dot grid
    angles. One angle has a measure of 45°.   to draw two
                                                 supplementary
                                                 angles, one of
                                                 which is 45°.
                                                 Do not use a
                                                 protractor.

Practice 7-3 Triangles

Find each missing angle measure.

1.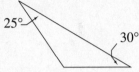

2.

3.

_____ _____ _____

Find the missing angle measures for each isosceles triangle.

4.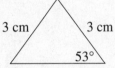

5.

6.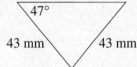

_____ _____ _____

Circle A, B, C, or D. Classify each triangle.

7. The measures of two angles are 45° and 45°.

    A. acute   **B.** right   **C.** obtuse   **D.** cannot be determined

8. The measures of two angles are 15° and 47°.

    A. acute   **B.** right   **C.** obtuse   **D.** cannot be determined

9. The measures of two angles are 53° and 76°.

    A. acute   **B.** right   **C.** obtuse   **D.** cannot be determined

10. The measure of one angle is 18°.

    A. acute   **B.** right   **C.** obtuse   **D.** cannot be determined

11. The measure of one angle is 90°.

    A. acute   **B.** right   **C.** obtuse   **D.** cannot be determined

12. The measure of one angle is 115°.

    A. acute   **B.** right   **C.** obtuse   **D.** cannot be determined

13. The measures of the angles of a triangle are 40°, 50°, and 90°.

    a. Classify the triangle by its angles. _____

    b. Can the triangle be equilateral? Why or why not? _____

    c. Can the triangle be isosceles? Why or why not? _____

    d. Can you classify the triangle by its sides? Why or why not? _____

    _____

Practice 7-4 Problem-Solving Strategy: Draw a Diagram

Use a diagram to help you solve each problem.

1. One angle of an isosceles triangle measures 56°. What are the measures of the other two angles?

   _____

2. The eight members of the Ping Pong Paddlers Club have a tournament in which every player plays a game against every other player. How many games are there in the tournament?

   _____

3. Moranda took a train trip to visit her cousin. By 10:15 the train had traveled 20 mi. By 10:30 the train had traveled an additional 10 mi. Moranda is now halfway to her cousin's town. At what time will she reach her cousin's town if the train's speed is constant? _____

4. Desmond's cat Calico likes to play on stairs. Starting at the bottom landing, Calico jumped up 4 steps, then down 2. Then Calico jumped up 5 steps and fell down 3. In two more jumps of 4 steps and then 5 steps, Calico reached the top of the stairs. How many stairs are in the staircase?_____

Use any strategy to solve each problem.

5. Carla is five years older than her sister Julie. The product of their ages is 234. How old is Julie?_____

6. Ms. Spender bought pens for her class. The pens all cost the same price. She bought as many pens as the cost (in cents) of each pen. She spent a total of $56.25. How many pens did she buy? _____

7. If the pattern at the right continues, how many dots will there be in the fifth figure?

   _____ •

                                                     1 dot   5 dots   12 dots

8. Frank, Bill, and Pam each ordered a salad at a restaurant. A spinach salad, a chef's salad, and a tuna salad were ordered. Bill did not order the spinach salad. Pam sat to the right of the one who ordered the spinach salad and to the left of the one who ordered the chef's salad. Who ordered which salad?

   _____

Practice 7-5 Congruent Triangles

1. List the pairs of triangles that appear to be congruent. _____

a.    b.    c.

d. 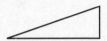   e.   f.

Complete. (Be sure that you name corresponding vertices in the same order.)

2. $\triangle ABC \cong$ _____

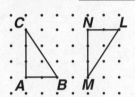

3. $\triangle ABC \cong$ _____

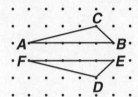

4. $\triangle ABC \cong$ _____

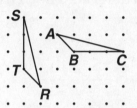

Write six congruences involving corresponding sides and angles for each pair of triangles.

5. $\triangle ABC \cong \triangle DEF$

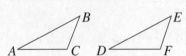

_____

_____

_____

6. $\triangle JKL \cong \triangle MNO$

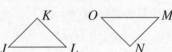

_____

_____

_____

7. $\triangle TUV \cong \triangle WXY$

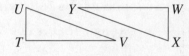

_____

_____

_____

Use the diagram at the right to complete each of the following.

8. a. $\angle ABC \cong$ _____

b. $\overline{AB} \cong$ _____

c. $\angle F \cong$ _____

9. a. $\triangle ABC \cong$ _____

b. $\triangle BAC \cong$ _____

c. $\triangle CAB \cong$ _____

10. Circle A, B, C, or D. $\triangle MNO$ and $\triangle TRS$ are congruent isosceles right triangles. $\angle N$ and $\angle R$ are right angles. Which angle or angles must be congruent to $\angle M$?

A. $\angle S$ only   **B.** $\angle S$ and $\angle T$ only   **C.** $\angle T$ only   **D.** $\angle O, \angle S,$ and $\angle T$

▄▄▄▄▄*Practice 7-6* Polygons and Quadrilaterals

Classify each polygon by the number of sides. State whether it appears to be a regular polygon.

1.

2.

3.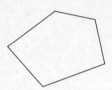

4.

_____ _____ _____ _____

Judging by appearance, state all correct names for each quadrilateral. Then circle the best name.

5.

6.

7.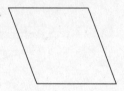

8.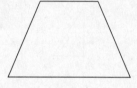

_____ _____ _____ _____

_____ _____ _____ _____

_____ _____ _____ _____

Draw each of the following on the dot grid.

9. a rectangle that is not a square

10. a rhombus with two right angles

11. a trapezoid with no right angles

12. Draw a pair of quadrilaterals where the angles of the first quadrilateral are congruent to the angles of the second quadrilateral. No side of one quadrilateral is to be congruent to any side of the other quadrilateral.

Practice 7-7 Circles

Name each of the following for circle _O_.

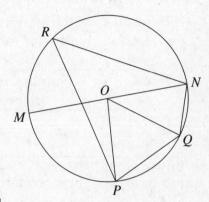

1. two chords

_____

2. three radii

_____

3. a diameter

_____

4. a central angle

_____

5. a semicircle

_____

6. two arcs

_____

7. the longest chord

_____

8. an inscribed quadrilateral

_____

Circle A, B, C, or D.

9. Which of the following is not an inscribed polygon?

  A.   **B.**   **C.**   **D.**

10. Which of the following shows an inscribed triangle that has a diameter as one of its sides?

  A.   **B.**   **C.**   **D.**

11. Which of the following polygons can be inscribed in a circle? There may be more than one choice. Make a sketch of each of the polygons that can be inscribed.

  A. Square   **B.** Rectangle   **C.** Parallelogram that is not a rectangle   **D.** Rhombus that is not a square

Practice 7-8 Circle Graphs

Use the data in Exercises 1, 2, and 3 to make circle graphs.

1. The data show the total number of space vehicles that either successfully reached or exceeded orbit around Earth.

Years	Number of Successful Space Launches
1957–1959	21
1960–1969	854
1970–1979	1,162
1980–1988	1,056

Source: *World Almanac and Book of Records*

2. The data represent the percent of private schools in the United States that have an annual tuition in each of the given ranges.

Annual Tuition	% of Private Schools
Less than $500	13
$500–$1,000	28
$1,001–$1,500	26
$1,501–$2,500	15
More than $2,500	18

Source: *National Center for Education Statistics, U.S. Dept. of Education*

3. The data represent a poll taken in a seventh-grade class.

Favorite Color for a Car	Number of 7th-Graders
Red	14
Blue	9
White	3
Green	1

Practice 7-9 Constructing Bisectors

Construct the perpendicular bisector of each segment.

1.

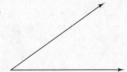

2.

Construct the bisector of each angle.

3.

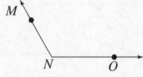

4.

5. Construct a segment with measure $\frac{3}{4}$ that of $\overline{AB}$.

6. Construct an angle with measure $\frac{1}{4}$ times that of $\angle MNO$.

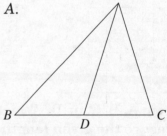

7. Draw an obtuse angle, $\angle RST$. Then construct and label its bisector $\overrightarrow{SV}$.

8. Draw an acute angle, $\angle MAT$. Then construct and label its bisector $\overrightarrow{AH}$.

9. **Circle A, B, C, or D.** $\overline{AD}$ bisects $\overline{BC}$ but does not bisect $\angle A$. Which of the following must be true?

   I. $\triangle ABD \cong \triangle ACD$ II. $\overline{AB} \cong \overline{AC}$

   III. $\angle BDA \cong \angle CDA$ IV. $\overline{BD} \cong \overline{CD}$

   A. I and IV   **B.** I, II, IV

   C. I and II   **D.** IV

10. Each square represents one acre of a farm. Draw 11 sections of fence along the dotted lines shown, so that four fields are formed, each containing four acres of land.

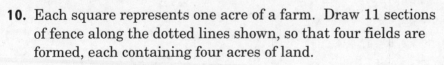

Practice 8-1 Estimating Length and Area

Estimate each length in inches.

1. _____
   _____

2. _____
   _____

3. _____
   _____

4. _____
   _____

Estimate each length in centimeters.

5. _____
   _____

6. _____
   _____

7. _____
   _____

8. _____
   _____

Suppose each square below is 1 cm by 1 cm. Estimate the area of each figure.

9.   10.   11.   12.

_____   _____   _____   _____

Circle A, B, C, or D. Which unit of measure would you use to measure the given length or area?

13. the height of a tree

   A. mm   **B.** cm   **C.** m   **D.** km

14. the perimeter of the cover of a book

   A. in.   **B.** ft   **C.** yd   **D.** mi

15. the area of an ocean

   A. ft^2 **B.** yd^2 **C.** in.^{2} **D.** mi^2

■■■*Practice 8-2* Area of Parallelograms

Choose a calculator, pencil and paper, or mental math to find the perimeter and area of each parallelogram.

1.

4 m
4 m

2.
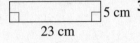
5 cm
23 cm

3.
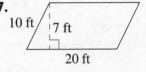
5 in. 4 in.
8 in.

4.
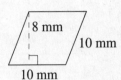
8 mm
10 mm
10 mm

_____ _____ _____ _____

5.
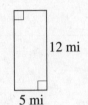
12 mi
5 mi

6.
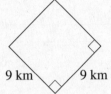
9 km   9 km

7.
10 ft   7 ft
20 ft

8.
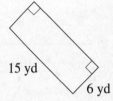
15 yd
6 yd

_____ _____ _____ _____

Find the area of each parallelogram.

9. rectangle: $l = 16$ mm, $w = 12$ mm

10. parallelogram: $b = 23$ km, $h = 14$ km

_____

11. square: $s = 27$ ft

12. rectangle: $l = 65$ mi, $w = 48$ mi

_____

13. parallelogram: $b = 19$ in., $h = 15$ in.

14. square: $s = 42$ m

_____

15. The perimeter of a square is 60 ft. What is the area?

16. The area of a rectangle is 320 m^2. The width of the rectangle is 16 m. What is the perimeter of the rectangle?

_____

Solve.

17. The area of a certain rectangle is 288 yd^2. The perimeter is 68 yd. If you double the length and width, what will be the area and perimeter of the new rectangle?

18. If you have 36 ft of fencing, what are the areas of the different rectangles you could enclose with the fencing? Consider only whole-number dimensions.

_____

_____

Practice 8-3 Area of Triangles and Trapezoids

Choose a calculator, paper and pencil, or mental math to find the area and perimeter of each figure.

1.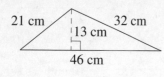
21 cm 32 cm
13 cm
46 cm

2.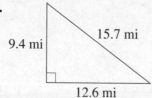
9.4 mi 15.7 mi
12.6 mi

3.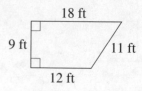
18 ft
9 ft 11 ft
12 ft

_____

4.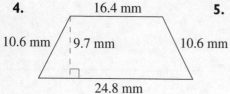
16.4 mm
10.6 mm 9.7 mm 10.6 mm
24.8 mm

5.
12.9 km 8.0 km
8.7 km
6.7 km
3.4 km

6.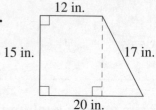
12 in.
15 in. 17 in.
20 in.

_____

7.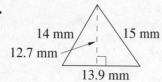
14 mm 15 mm
12.7 mm
13.9 mm

8.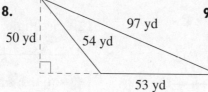
50 yd 97 yd
54 yd
53 yd

9.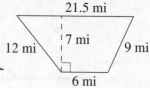
21.5 mi
12 mi 7 mi 9 mi
6 mi

_____

10.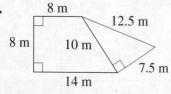
8 m
12.5 m
8 m 10 m
7.5 m
14 m

11.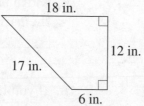
18 in.
12 in.
17 in.
6 in.

12.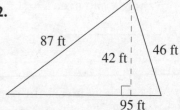
87 ft 46 ft
42 ft
95 ft

_____

Solve.

13. The area of a triangle is 6 square units. Both the height and the length of the base are whole numbers. What are the possible lengths and heights?

_____

14. A trapezoid has an area of 4 square units, and a height of 1 unit. What are the possible whole-number lengths for the bases?

_____

Practice 8-4 Circumference and Area of Circles

Find the circumference and area of each circle to the nearest tenth.

1.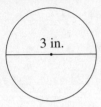
3 in.

2.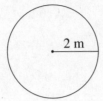
2 m

3.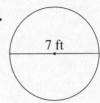
7 ft

4.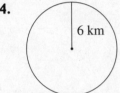
6 km

5.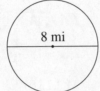
8 mi

6.
15 in.

7.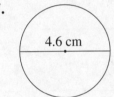
4.6 cm

8.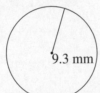
9.3 mm

9.
47 km

10.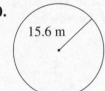
15.6 m

11.
17 yd

12.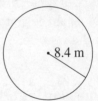
8.4 m

Given the circumference of a circle, find the radius to the nearest tenth.

13. $C = 80$ km   **14.** $C = 92$ ft   **15.** $C = 420$ in.   **16.** $C = 700$ km

_____   _____   _____   _____

17. The radius of the large circle is 8 in. The radius of each of the smaller circles is 1 in. Find the area of the shaded region to the nearest unit.

_____

▬▬Practice 8-5 Exploring Square Roots

Find each of the following. Use mental math as much as possible.

1. 6^2 _____
2. 1^2 _____
3. $\sqrt{64}$ _____
4. 4^2 _____

5. $\sqrt{81}$ _____
6. 5^2 _____
7. $\sqrt{100}$ _____
8. 2^2 _____

9. $\sqrt{144}$ _____
10. 3^2 _____
11. 9^2 _____
12. $\sqrt{121}$ _____

13. $\sqrt{1}$ _____
14. $\sqrt{36}$ _____
15. 13^2 _____
16. 7^2 _____

17. 14^2 _____
18. $\sqrt{169}$ _____
19. 15^2 _____
20. $\sqrt{25}$ _____

21. 16^2 _____
22. 10^2 _____
23. $\sqrt{16}$ _____
24. $\sqrt{256}$ _____

25. $\sqrt{9}$ _____
26. 12^2 _____
27. $\sqrt{196}$ _____
28. 8^2 _____

29. $\sqrt{49}$ _____
30. $\sqrt{225}$ _____
31. 11^2 _____
32. $\sqrt{4}$ _____

Find the length of a side of a square with the given area.

33. 64 km^2
34. 81 m^2
35. 121 ft^2
36. 4 mi^2

_____ _____ _____ _____

37. 225 in.^2
38. 196 yd^2
39. 169 cm^2
40. 144 mm^2

_____ _____ _____ _____

Solve.

41. The square of a certain number is the same as three times the number. What is the number?

_____

42. The area of a square lawn is 196 yd^2. What is the perimeter of the lawn?

_____

Find two consecutive whole numbers that each square root is between.

43. $\sqrt{80}$
44. $\sqrt{56}$
45. $\sqrt{130}$
46. $\sqrt{150}$

_____ _____ _____ _____

47. $\sqrt{70}$
48. $\sqrt{190}$
49. $\sqrt{204}$
50. $\sqrt{159}$

_____ _____ _____ _____

Practice 8-6 *Exploring the Pythagorean Theorem*

Find the missing side length.

1.

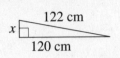

122 cm

x

120 cm

_____

2.

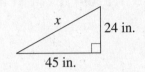

x

24 in.

45 in.

_____

3.

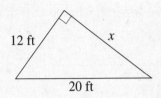

12 ft

x

20 ft

_____

4.

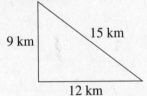

60 m

x

65m

_____

5.

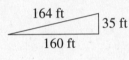

36 yd

105 yd

x

_____

6.

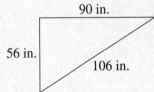

82 mi

80 mi

x

_____

Determine whether each triangle is a right triangle. Explain your answer.

7.

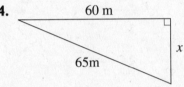

9 km

15 km

12 km

_____

8.

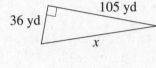

164 ft

35 ft

160 ft

_____

9.

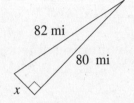

90 in.

56 in.

106 in.

_____

10.

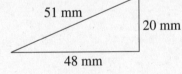

51 mm

20 mm

48 mm

_____

11.

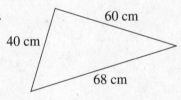

60 cm

40 cm

68 cm

_____

12.

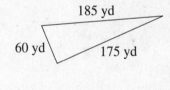

185 yd

60 yd

175 yd

_____

13. A guy wire runs from the top of a tower to the ground, where the wire is anchored 11 ft from the tower. If the guy wire is 61 ft long, how tall is the tower?

_____

14. The base of a ladder is placed 6 ft from the bottom of the house. The ladder reaches 8 ft up the house. How long is the ladder?

_____

15. Ishmael owns a triangular piece of land. The sides of the land measure 6 mi by 8 mi by 9 mi. Is the land a right triangle?

_____

16. A park along a river is in the shape of a triangle. The lengths of the sides of the park are 330 yd by 1,800 yd by 1,830 yd. Does the park form a right triangle?

_____

Practice 8-7 Applying the Pythagorean Theorem

The lengths of two sides of a right triangle are given. Find the length of the third side to the nearest tenth of a unit.

1. legs: 5 ft and 12 ft

_____

2. legs: 13 cm and 9 cm

_____

3. leg: 7 m; hypotenuse: 14 m

_____

4. legs: 17 ft and 6 ft

_____

5. legs: 11 cm and 21 cm

_____

6. leg: 15 m; hypotenuse: 20 m

_____

Find the missing side length to the nearest tenth.

7.
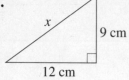
_____

8.
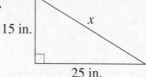
_____

9.
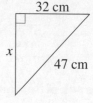
_____

10.

_____

11.
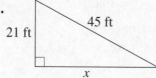
_____

12.
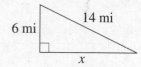
_____

13.
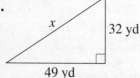
_____

14.

_____

15.
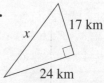
_____

Solve.

16. A playground is 50 yd by 50 yd. Amy walked across the playground from one corner to the opposite corner. How far did she walk?

_____

17. A 70-ft ladder is mounted 10 ft above the ground on a fire truck. The bottom of the ladder is 40 ft from the wall of a building. The top of the ladder is touching the building. How high off the ground is the top of the ladder?

_____

Practice 8-8 *Three-Dimensional Figures*

Give the best name for each three-dimensional figure.
Describe the base.

1.

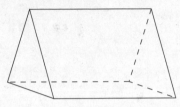

_____

_____

2.

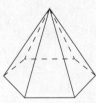

_____

_____

3.

_____

_____

4.

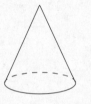

_____

_____

5.

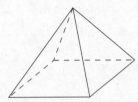

_____

_____

6.

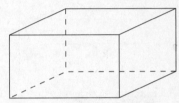

_____

_____

Use the figure at the right for Exercises 7–8.

7. Name three pairs of parallel edges.

_____

8. Name four edges that intersect $\overline{ML}$.

_____

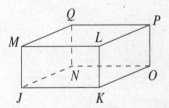

Draw each figure named.

9. a triangular pyramid

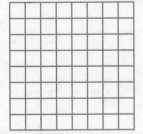

10. a square prism

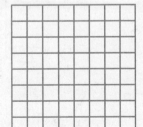

Name _____ Class _____ Date _____

■■■■Practice 8-9 *Surface Area of Prisms and Cylinders*

Choose a calculator, paper and pencil, or mental math to find the surface area of each rectangular prism.

1.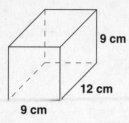

9 cm

12 cm

9 cm

_____

2.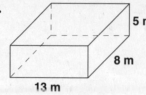

5 m

8 m

13 m

_____

3.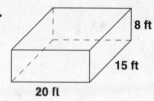

8 ft

15 ft

20 ft

_____

4.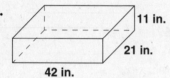

11 in.

21 in.

42 in.

_____

5.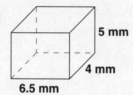

5 mm

4 mm

6.5 mm

_____

6.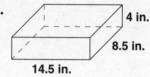

4 in.

8.5 in.

14.5 in.

_____

Choose a calculator or paper and pencil to find the surface area of each cylinder. Round to the nearest unit.

7.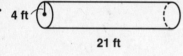

4 ft

21 ft

_____

8.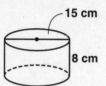

15 cm

8 cm

_____

9.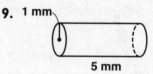

1 mm

5 mm

_____

10.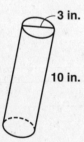

3 in.

10 in.

_____

11.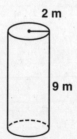

2 m

9 m

_____

12.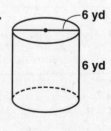

6 yd

6 yd

_____

Circle A, B, C, or D. The surface area of each rectangular prism is given. Find each missing measure.

13. 254 in.^{2}

  A. 8   **B.** 4

  C. 2   **D.** 4.3

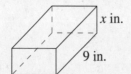

x in.

9 in.

7 in.

14. 1,230 cm^2

  A. 10   **B.** 9.1

  C. 20   **D.** 40

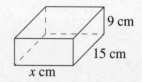

9 cm

15 cm

x cm

Name_____ Class_____ Date_____

Practice 8-10 *Volume of Rectangular Prisms and Cylinders*

Choose a calculator, paper and pencil, or mental math to find each volume to the nearest tenth.

1. 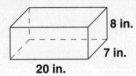 8 in. 7 in. 20 in.

_____

2. 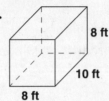 8 ft 10 ft 8 ft

_____

3. 6 ft 15 ft

_____

4. 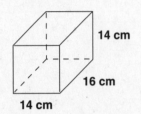 14 cm 16 cm 14 cm

_____

5. 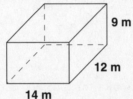 9 m 12 m 14 m

_____

6. 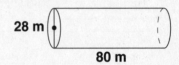 28 m 80 m

_____

7. 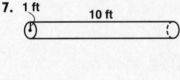 1 ft 10 ft

_____

8. 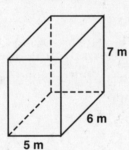 7 m 6 m 5 m

_____

9. 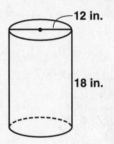 12 in. 18 in.

_____

Circle A, B, C, or D. Which expression represents the volume of each rectangular prism?

10.

A. $7x^3$ **B.** $8x^3$

C. $8x$ **D.** $7x$

x

$4x$

$2x$

11.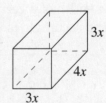

A. $10x^3$ **B.** $10x$

C. $36x^3$ **D.** $36x$

$3x$

$4x$

$3x$

Practice 8-11 *Problem-Solving Strategy:*
Guess and Test

Solve using the Guess and Test strategy.

1. The volume of a cube is 79,507 in.^{3}.
   What is the length of each edge of the cube? _____

2. What are two whole numbers whose product is 294 and
   whose quotient is 6?

3. Tickets for a concert sold for $8 for floor seats and $6 for
   balcony seats. For one performance, 400 tickets were sold,
   bringing in $2,888. How many of each ticket were sold?

   _____

   _____

4. Aaron bought 6 books and 2 notebooks for $46.86. Erin bought
   2 books and 6 notebooks for $27.78. How much does one book
   cost?

   _____

Solve if possible. If not, tell what information is needed.

5. Find the volume of a rectangular prism. The width is half the
   length. The height is twice the length.

   _____

   _____

6. Sal raises pigs and chickens. She has 420 creatures, with a
   total of 1,240 legs. How many pigs does Sal raise?

   _____

7. The width of a rectangle is 6 in. less than the length. The area
   of the rectangle is 135 in.^{2}. Find the length and width.

   _____

8. A cube is filled with water that has a volume of 4,096 cm^3.
   What is the length of each edge of the cube?

   _____

9. Tom is 26 years older than Paul. The product of their ages
   is 560. How old is Paul?

   _____

▰▰▰ *Practice 9-1* Experimental Probability

Suppose you observe the color of socks worn by students in
your class. Twelve have white, four have black, three have
blue, and one has red. Write each probability as a fraction in
simplest form.

1. P(white) _____

2. P(red) _____

3. P(blue) _____

4. P(black) _____

5. P(yellow) _____

6. P(black or red) _____

Use the data in the table at the right for Exercises 7–12.
Write each probability as a percent.

7. P(fruit) _____

8. P(candy) _____

9. P(pretzels) _____

10. P(cookies) _____

11. P(not fruit) _____

12. P(candy or chips) _____

Favorite Snack
Survey Results

Snack	Number of Students
Fruit	8
Candy	2
Pretzels	3
Chips	7
Cookies	5

13. Do an experiment to find the probability that a word chosen
randomly in a book is the word *the*. How many words did you
look at to find P(the)? What is P(the)?

_____

14. **Circle A, B, C, or D.** Suppose each of the following are the
results of tossing a coin. Which result suggests an
experimental probability of 60% for heads?

   A. head, tail, tail, tail, head

   B. head, head, tail, head, head

   C. tail, tail, head, head, tail

   D. head, tail, head, tail, head

Solve.

15. The probability that a twelve-year-old is taller than 60 inches
is 25%. Suppose you measure 300 twelve-year-old boys. About
how many do you think will be taller than 60 inches?

_____

16. **a.** A quality control inspector found flaws in 13 out of 150
   sweaters. Find the probability that a sweater has a flaw.
   Round to the nearest tenth of a percent. _____

   b. Suppose the company produces 500 sweaters a day. How
   many will not have flaws? _____

■■■■■Practice 9-2 Problem-Solving Strategy:
Simulate a Problem

Describe a simulation you could use to solve each problem.

1. A grocery store is running a contest. Every time you enter the store, you receive a card with the letter W, I, N, E, or R. You have an equally likely chance of receiving any one card. To win a prize, you must spell WINNER by collecting the cards. How many times will you have to enter the store to win a prize?

   _____

   _____

2. A sugarless-gum company wraps its product in a piece of paper with one of the digits 1 to 6 on the paper. When you collect wrappers that contain all 6 digits, you win a prize. Use a number cube to help you decide how many pieces of gum you will need to buy in order to get all 6 digits.

   _____

   _____

Use any strategy to solve each problem. Show your work.

3. In 1960, the submarine *Triton* traveled 36,014 miles journeying around the world. If the trip took 76 days, how many miles did the Triton average each day?

   _____

4. After working for a company for a year, Melanie received a 10% raise in her salary. Later, the entire company took a 10% cut in pay because of budget difficulties. If Melanie started working at $2,000 a month, what would she now be receiving?

   _____

5. At the mall on Saturday, Suki bought a pair of blue jeans for $15.55 and some books for $8.53. For lunch she spent $1.50 on juice and $3.25 on a sandwich. When she left the mall she had $5.27 left. How much money did Suki take to the mall?

   _____

6. Mari plans to make a doll's quilt with 16 squares. Half of the squares will be solid red. The rest of the squares will be half calico print and half white. If each square is 9 inches on a side, how many square feet of each type of fabric will she need?

   _____

Practice 9-3 *Theoretical Probability and Proportional Reasoning*

A spinner numbered 1 through 10 is spun. Each outcome is equally likely. Write each probability as a fraction, decimal, and percent.

1. $P(9)$
2. P(even)
3. P(number greater than 0)
4. P(multiple of 4)

_____ _____ _____ _____

There are eight blue marbles, nine orange marbles, and six yellow marbles in a bag. It is equally likely that any marble is drawn from the bag.

5. Find the probability of drawing a blue marble. _____

6. Find the probability of drawing a yellow marble. _____

7. What marble could you add or remove so that the probability of drawing a blue marble is $\frac{1}{3}$?

_____

Suppose you have a box that contains 12 slips of paper as shown. Each slip of paper is equally likely to be drawn. Find the probability of each event.

red	blue	yellow	blue
yellow	red	blue	red
red	red	red	yellow

8. P(red)
9. P(blue)
10. P(yellow)

_____ _____ _____

11. P(red) + P(blue)
12. P(red) + P(yellow)
13. P(blue) + P(yellow)

_____ _____ _____

14. P(red or blue)
15. P(red or yellow)
16. P(blue or yellow)

_____ _____ _____

17. P(not red)
18. P(not blue)
19. P(not yellow)

_____ _____ _____

In a raffle, there will be 3 prizes for every 1,000 tickets sold.

20. What is the probability of winning? _____

21. What is the probability of not winning? _____

Name _____ Class _____ Date _____

■■■ *Practice 9-4* *Sample Spaces*

Solve the problem.

1. A theater uses a letter to show which row a seat is in, and a number to show the column the seat is in. If there are eight rows and ten columns, make a table to show the sample space for the seats.

A coin is tossed three times.

2. **a.** Draw a tree diagram that shows all the possible outcomes of how the coin will land.

    b. Find the probability that the coin will land heads up all three times or tails up all three times. _____

3. A pizza company makes pizza in three different sizes, small, medium, and large. There are four possible toppings, pepperoni, sausage, green pepper, and mushroom. How many different kinds of pizza with one topping are available? _____

Susan, Joanne, and Diane are triplets. Susan has red, blue, green, and yellow sweaters. Joanne has green, red, purple, and white sweaters. Diane's sweaters are red, blue, purple, and mauve. Each girl has only one sweater of each color, and will pick a sweater to wear at random. Find each probability.

4. *P*(each girl chooses a different color)

_____

5. *P*(each girl chooses the same color)

_____

6. *P*(two girls choose the same color, and the third chooses a different color)

_____

7. *P*(each girl chooses a red sweater)

_____

Practice 9-5 Independent and Dependent Events

Each letter in the word MASSACHUSETTS is written on a card. You are equally likely to get any card.

1. What is the probability of selecting two S's if the first card is replaced before selecting the second card?

   _____

2. What is the probability of selecting two S's if the first card is not replaced before selecting the second card?

   _____

You roll a fair number cube. What is the probability of each of the events?

3. $P(3, \text{then } 5)$

   _____

4. $P(2, \text{then } 2)$

   _____

5. $P(5, \text{then } 4, \text{then } 6)$

   _____

6. $P(6, \text{then } 0)$

   _____

7. $P(9, \text{then } 4)$

   _____

8. $P(2, \text{then } 1, \text{then } 5)$

   _____

Four girls and eight boys are running for president or vice president of the Student Council.

9. Find the probability that two boys are elected.

   _____

10. Find the probability that two girls are elected.

    _____

11. Find the probability that the president is a boy and the vice president is a girl.

    _____

12. Find the probability that the president is a girl and the vice president is a boy.

    _____

The box contains ten balls, numbered 1 through 10. Marisha reaches in without looking and draws a ball. Then Penney draws a ball without looking. Find each probability.

13. $P(\text{the sum of the numbers is even})$

    _____

14. $P(\text{the sum of the numbers is odd})$

    _____

15. $P(\text{the sum of the numbers is 7})$

    _____

16. $P(\text{the sum of the numbers is 20})$

    _____

17. $P(\text{the sum of the numbers is prime})$

    _____

18. $P(\text{the sum of the numbers is greater than 8})$

    _____

Practice 9-6 Permutations

Start with the letters in the word STEP.

1. Make an organized list of all the possible four-letter permutations of the letters.

2. How many of the permutations form real words? _____

Use the counting principle to find the number of permutations for each group of letters. Use all the letters.

3. C, H, A, I, R   4. L, I, G, H, T, S   5. C, O, M, P, U, T, E, R

_____   _____   _____

Find the number of three-letter permutations of each group.

6. A, P, Q, M   7. L, S, U, V, R,   8. M, B, T, O, D, K

_____   _____   _____

Solve.

9. Suppose that first, second, and third place winners of a contest are to be selected from eight students who entered. In how many ways can the winners be chosen? _____

10. Antonio has nine different sweatshirts that he can wear for his job doing yard work. He has three pairs of jeans and two pairs of sweatpants. How many different outfits can Antonio wear for the yard work? _____

11. Ramona has a combination lock for her bicycle. She knows the numbers are 20, 41, and 6, but she can't remember the order. How many different arrangements are possible?

_____

12. Travis is planting 5 rose bushes along a fence. Each rose bush has a different flower color: red, yellow, pink, peach, and white. If he wants to plant 3 rose bushes in between white and yellow rose bushes, in how many ways can he plant the 5 rose bushes?

_____

Practice 9-7 Combinations

Find the number of combinations.

1. Choose 3 people from 4.

_____

2. Choose 4 people from 6.

_____

Use the numbers 3, 5, 8, 10, 12, 15, 20. Make a list of all the combinations.

3. 2 even numbers

_____

4. 3 odd numbers

_____

5. 1 even, 1 odd

_____

_____

6. any 2 numbers

_____

_____

_____

7. You just bought five new books to read. You want to take two of them with you on vacation. In how many ways can you choose two books to take? _____

Charmayne is organizing a track meet. There are 4 runners in her class. Each runner must compete one-on-one against each of the other runners in her class.

8. How many races must Charmayne schedule? _____

9. Must Charmayne schedule permutations or combinations? _____

A committee for the end-of-year party is composed of four eighth graders and three seventh graders. A three-member subcommittee is formed.

10. How many different combinations of eighth graders could there be if there are three eighth graders on the subcommittee?

_____

11. How many different combinations of seventh graders could there be if the subcommittee consists of three seventh graders?

_____

12. Find the probability that all 3 members on the subcommittee are eighth graders.

_____

13. Find the probability that all 3 members on the subcommittee are seventh graders.

_____

Course 2 Chapter 9

■■■■Practice 9-8 Estimating Population Size

Workers at a state park caught, tagged, and set free the species shown at the right. Later that same year, the workers caught the number of animals shown in the table below, and counted the tagged animals. Estimate the park population of each species.

Tagged Animals	
Bears	12
Squirrels	50
Raccoons	23
Rabbits	42
Trout	46
Owls	24
Foxes	14
Skunks	21

	Caught	Counted Tagged	Estimated Population
1. Bears	30	9	
2. Squirrels	1,102	28	
3. Raccoons	412	10	
4. Rabbits	210	2	
5. Trout	318	25	
6. Owls	117	10	
7. Foxes	54	9	
8. Skunks	45	6	

Imagine that you are working in a National Park. One season, you tag 100 animals. Estimate the total population for each of the following samples.

9. 23 out of 100 animals are tagged

_____

10. 12 out of 75 animals are tagged

_____

11. 8 out of 116 animals are tagged

_____

12. 5 out of 63 animals are tagged

_____

13. 4 out of 83 animals are tagged

_____

14. 3 out of 121 animals are tagged

_____

15. 83 out of 125 animals are tagged

_____

16. 7 out of 165 animals are tagged

_____

■■■ *Practice 10-1* Number Patterns

Identify each sequence as arithmetic, geometric, or neither. Write a rule to describe each arithmetic and geometric sequence.

1. 2, 6, 18, 54, . . .

_____

_____

2. 5, −10, 20, −40, . . .

_____

_____

3. 3, 5, 7, 9, . . .

_____

_____

4. 5, 6, 8, 11, 15, . . .

_____

_____

5. 1, 2, 6, 24, . . .

_____

_____

6. 17, 16, 15, 14, . . .

_____

_____

7. 50, −50, 50, −50, . . .

_____

_____

8. 1, 2, 4, 5, 10, 11, 22, . . .

_____

_____

Circle A, B, C, or D. Find the next three numbers in each sequence.

9. 15, −14, 13, −12, . . .

  A. −8, 11, −14   **B.** −10, 17, −21

  C. −11, 10, −9   **D.** 11, −10, 9

10. 243, 81, 27, . . .

  A. 9, 3, 1   **B.** 9, 27, 81

  C. 27, 81, 243   **D.** 9, 3, 0

11. 5, 12, 26, . . .

  A. 52, 104, 208   **B.** 33, 40, 47

  C. 54, 110, 222   **D.** 40, 54, 68

12. 2, 5, 9, 14, . . .

  A. 19, 24, 29   **B.** 20, 27, 35

  C. 17, 20, 23   **D.** 20, 26, 32

Write the first five terms in the sequence described by the rule. Identify the sequence as arithmetic, geometric, or neither.

13. Start with 2 and multiply by −3 repeatedly.

_____

14. Start with 27 and add −9 repeatedly.

_____

15. Start with 18 and multiply by 0.1, then by 0.2, then by 0.3, and so on.

_____

Practice 10-2 Scientific Notation

Write each number in scientific notation.

1. 73,000,000

2. 4,300

3. 510

4. 56,870

_____

5. 68,900

6. 98,000,000,000

7. 4,890,000

8. 38

_____

9. 120,000

10. 543,000

11. 27

12. 54,000

_____

Write each number in standard form.

13. 5.7×10^6

14. 2.45×10^8

15. 4.706×10^{11}

_____

16. 8×10^1

17. 7.2×10^3

18. 1.63×10^{12}

_____

19. 8.03×10^{14}

20. 3.26×10^4

21. 5.179×10^5

_____

Write each number in scientific notation.

22. One type of roundworm can lay 200,000 eggs each day.

_____

23. The nose of a German shepherd dog has about 220 million cells that are used in picking out smells.

_____

24. In a given day, a total of 15,000 tons of potatoes are consumed by the people of Britain.

_____

25. A computer microchip can perform about 400,000 operations each second.

_____

26. The brain contains about 100 trillion nerve connections.

_____

27. During an average life span, the human heart will beat about 2,800,000,000 times.

_____

28. The volume of the Grand Coulee Dam is about 10.6 million cubic yards.

_____

29. A second has been defined as the time it takes for an atom of a particular metal to vibrate 9,192,631,770 times.

_____

Practice 10-3 Problem-Solving Strategy: Solve a Simpler Problem

Solve using a simpler problem.

1. A school's gym lockers are numbered from 1 to 125. How many locker numbers contain the digit 4? _____

2. How many diagonals can you draw in an 8-sided regular polygon? _____

3. Sixty-four players signed up for a tennis tournament. A player is eliminated upon losing a match. How many matches must be scheduled to determine the tournament champion? _____

4. Study the dot patterns. How many dots will the 12th pattern have? _____

Choose any strategy to solve each problem.

5. Andy, Bryan, and Samantha are friends. One is an architect, another is a teacher, and another is a baker. The architect, who lives next door to Bryan, took Samantha to lunch today. Before lunch, Samantha bought bread from the baker. Who is the baker? _____

6. Study the dot patterns. Draw the next four patterns.

7. The sum of three children's ages is 21 and the product of their ages is 336. How old are the children? _____

Solve or tell what information is needed to solve.

8. Al saves $4 each week. He has $64 already saved for a special bike. He also received $20 for his birthday. How many more weeks does he need to save before he can buy the bike?

_____

Practice 10-4 *Simple and Compound Interest*

Choose a calculator or pencil and paper to find the simple interest earned by each account.

1. $700 principal
   3% interest rate
   2 years

   _____

2. $950 principal
   8% interest rate
   5 years

   _____

3. $5,000 principal
   6.5% interest rate
   3 years

   _____

Choose a spreadsheet or calculator to find the balance of each account earning compound interest.

4. $800 principal
   6% interest rate
   9 years

   _____

5. $5,200 principal
   5% interest rate
   4 years

   _____

6. $3,500 principal
   4.5% interest rate
   10 years

   _____

Circle A, B, C, or D. Which expression yields the greatest amount?

7. **A.** $400(1 + .06)^3$ **B.** $400(1 + .07)^3$
   C. $400(1 + .08)^3$ **D.** $400(1 + .09)^3$

8. **A.** $500(1 + .06)^2$ **B.** $450(1 + .07)^2$
   C. $250(1 + .06)^3$ **D.** $200(1 + .07)^3$

9. **A.** $100(1 + .06)^2$ **B.** $100(1 + .05)^2$
   C. $100(1 + .005)^{24}$ **D.** $100(1 + .006)^{18}$

10. **A.** $200(1 + .06)^{10}$ **B.** $200(1 + .006)^{120}$
    C. $200(1 + .05)^{15}$ **D.** $200(1 + .006)^{150}$

Choose a calculator or a computer. Use exponents.

11. You deposit $600. The account pays 5% interest compounded annually. How much money is in the account at the end of 4 years?

    _____

12. You deposit $2,000 in an account that pays 6% interest compounded annually. How much money is in the account at the end of 12 years?

    _____

13. You invest $5,000 in an account earning simple interest. The balance after 6 years is $6,200. What is the interest rate?

    _____

Practice 10-5 Using Tables, Rules, and Graphs

The graph at the right shows the relationship between distance and time for a car driven at a constant speed.

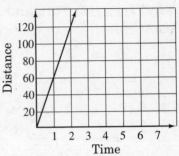

1. What is the speed? _____

2. Is this a function relationship? _____

3. If this is a function, write a rule to represent it.
   _____

4. Make a table for the function, listing six input/output pairs.

5. The function machine at the right shows your hourly wages. What are your wages if you work 5 h?
   _____

6. Write a rule for the function. _____

7. For the function machine at the right, what input would give an output of $15.45? _____

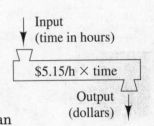

Input
(time in hours)

$5.15/h × time

Output
(dollars)

A car travels at a constant speed of 55 mi/h. Complete the table to show the time and distance the car would travel.

	Time (h)	Distance (mi)
8.		55
9.		96.25
10.	2.5	
11.		178.75

Circle A, B, C, or D. Which value could *not* be an output for the given function if only whole numbers are used as inputs?

12. $3x + 8$

   A. 6   **B.** 14

   C. 11   **D.** 8

13. $2x - 1$

   A. 3   **B.** 21

   C. 8   **D.** 11

Practice 10-6 Function Rules

Find $f(1)$, $f(2)$, $f(3)$, and $f(4)$ for the function represented by each rule.

1. $f(n) = 2n$ **2.** $f(n) = n + 4$ **3.** $f(n) = n^2 - 1$ **4.** $f(n) = -2n$

_____   _____   _____   _____

5. $f(n) = 3n + 1$ **6.** $f(n) = 8 - 3n$ **7.** $f(n) = 6 + 4n$ **8.** $f(n) = n - 5$

_____   _____   _____   _____

9. $f(n) = 2n + 7$ **10.** $f(n) = -5n + 6$ **11.** $f(n) = 3n + 9$ **12.** $f(n) = \frac{n}{2}$

_____   _____   _____   _____

Write a rule for the function represented by each table.

13.

n	$f(n)$
1	6
2	7
3	8
4	9

14.

n	$f(n)$
1	4
2	8
3	12
4	16

15.

n	$f(n)$
1	-6
2	-9
3	-12
4	-15

_____   _____   _____

16.

n	$f(n)$
1	5
2	7
3	9
4	11

17.

n	$f(n)$
1	4
2	7
3	10
4	13

18.

n	$f(n)$
1	-1
2	-3
3	-5
4	-7

_____   _____   _____

Circle A, B, C, or D. If input values must be given in whole numbers, which function would *not* produce the given number as an output?

19. 9

   A. $f(n) = n^2$ **B.** $f(n) = \frac{2}{3}n - 1$

   C. $f(n) = n^2 - 1$ **D.** $f(n) = 2n + 1$

20. -1

   A. $f(n) = n - 1$ **B.** $f(n) = n^2$

   C. $f(n) = n^2 - 1$ **D.** $f(n) = 2n - 7$

Practice 10-7 Interpreting Graphs

**Graphs I through VI represent one of the six situations
described below. Match each graph with the appropriate
situation.**

I.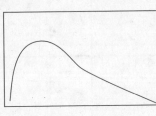

II.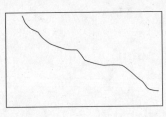

III.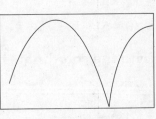

IV.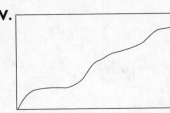

V.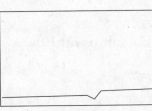

VI.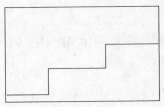

1. temperature as the weather changes from rainy to snowy

____

2. number of fish caught per hour on a bad fishing day _____

3. total rainfall during a rainy day _____

4. speed of a car starting from a stop sign and then approaching a
   stoplight _____

5. height of a cricket as it jumps _____

6. total amount of money spent over time during a trip to the mall

____

Sketch a graph to represent each situation.

7. The speed of a runner in a 1-mi race.

8. The height above ground of the air
   valve on a tire of a bicycle ridden on
   flat ground. (You can model this using
   a coin.)

Practice 11-1 Graphing Points in Four Quadrants

Name the point with the given coordinates.

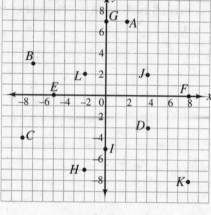

1. (−2, 2) _____   2. (8, 0) _____

3. (4, −3) _____   4. (−7, 3) _____

5. (0, −5) _____   6. (−8, −4) _____

Write the coordinates of each point.

7. E _____   8. A _____

9. H _____   10. K _____

11. G _____   12. J _____

Identify the quadrant in which each point lies.

13. (−4, 3) ___   14. (7, 21) ___   15. (5, −8) ___   16. (−2, −7) ___

In each drawing, a robot arm must move the black peg onto the white square, but the peg must be moved around—not over—the solid walls. List the coordinates of the vertices of a path the robot arm might follow to move the peg.

17.

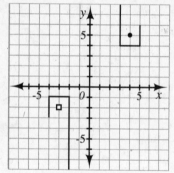

_____

_____

18.

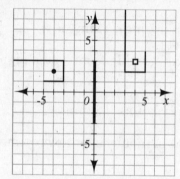

_____

_____

19. Circle A, B, C, or D. Which of the following groups of ordered pairs are *not* the vertices of a square?

A. (3, 0), (0, 3), (−3, 0), (0, −3)

B. (0, 0), (4, 0), (4, 4), (0, 4)

C. (3, 3), (−3, 3), (5, −5), (−5, 5)

D. (6, 6), (−6, 6), (−6, −6), (6, −6)

Practice 11-2 Graphing Linear Equations

Tell whether each ordered pair is a solution of $y = x - 4$.

1. $(0, -4)$ _____   **2.** $(5, -1)$ _____   **3.** $(-3, -7)$ _____   **4.** $(-7, -3)$ _____

On which of the following lines does each point lie? (A point may lie on more than one line.)

$$\text{I. } y = x + 5$$
$$\text{II. } y = -x + 7$$
$$\text{III. } y = 2x - 1$$

5. $(0, 5)$ _____   **6.** $(1, 6)$ _____   **7.** $\frac{8}{3}, \frac{13}{3}$ _____   **8.** $(0, -1)$ _____

9. $(4, 9)$ _____   **10.** $(4, 3)$ _____   **11.** $(-2, -5)$ _____   **12.** $(-8, 15)$ _____

Graph each equation on a coordinate plane.

13. $y = 3x - 1$ **14.** $y = -2x + 1$ **15.** $y = 2x - 4$

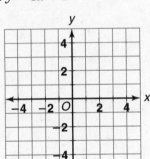   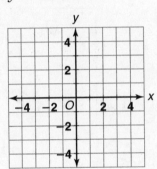   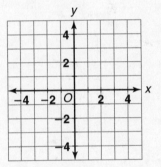

16. Circle A, B, C, or D. The graph of which equation passes through the fourth quadrant?

   A. $y = x + 1$ **B.** $y = -x$ **C.** $y = x$ **D.** $y = 2x$

17. Use the graph at the right to determine the coordinates of the point that is a solution of the equations of lines p and q.

_____

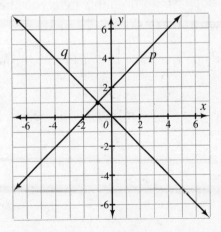

Practice 11-3 Finding the Slope of a Line

Find the slope of each line.

1. _____

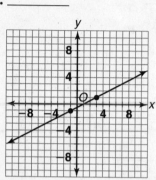

2. _____

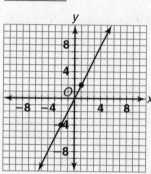

3. _____

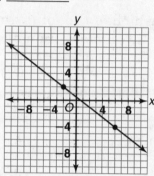

Use the coordinate plane provided to graph the given points.
Determine the slope of the line through the points.

4. $(-4, 6), (8, 4)$ _____

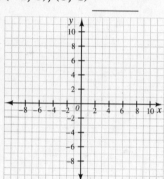

5. $(-1, 3), (4, 6)$ _____

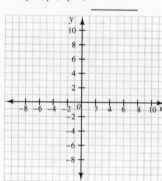

6. $(-2, 3), (4, -6)$ _____

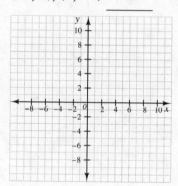

7. Which slope would it be easiest to push a heavy cart up, $\frac{1}{2}$, $\frac{1}{6}$, 3, or 5? _____

8. Which slope would probably give you the greatest speed down a hill when you are skiing, $\frac{1}{8}$, $\frac{1}{4}$, 1, or 2? _____

9. Which slope would be the most dangerous for a roofer trying to repair a roof, $\frac{1}{16}$, $\frac{1}{10}$, $\frac{1}{2}$, or $\frac{3}{2}$? _____

10. Which of the slopes from Exercise 9 would be the easiest for the roofer? _____

Practice 11-4 Exploring Nonlinear Relationships

Match each graph with an equation.

1.

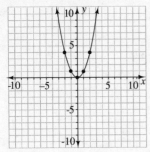

_____

2.

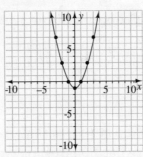

_____

3.

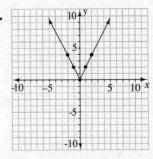

_____

4.

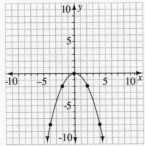

_____

5.

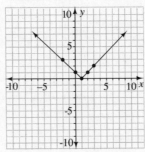

_____

6.

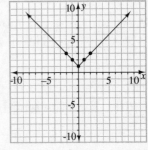

_____

A. $y = |x - 1|$

B. $y = x^2$

C. $y = -\frac{1}{2}x^2$

D. $y = |x| + 1$

E. $y = |2x|$

F. $y = x^2 - 1$

7. a. Complete the table below for the equation $y = x^2 + 2$.

x	-3	-2	-1	0	1	2	3
y							

b. Graph the ordered pairs and connect the points as smoothly as possible.

c. Describe how this graph is different from the graph of $y = x^2$.

_____

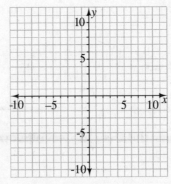

■■■■Practice 11-5 Problem-Solving Stategy:
Write an Equation

Write an equation to solve each problem. Show your work.

1. In a pet store the number of dogs is 12 more than three times the number of cats. If the pet store has 21 dogs, how many cats does it have?

   _____

2. In the pet store the number of birds is 10 less than twice the number of rabbits. If the pet store has 56 birds, how many rabbits does it have?

   _____

3. A sweater cost $12 more than a shirt. Together they cost $46. What was the price of the shirt?

   _____

4. The perimeter of a rectangle is 84 cm. The length is twice the width. Find the length and width.

   _____

5. Mark and Melinda collect baseball caps. Mark has 7 more than Melinda. Together, they have 115 caps. How many baseball caps does each of them have?

   _____

Use any strategy to solve each problem.

6. Lydia sold $\frac{4}{5}$ of her candles to raise money for the band. She has 8 candles left. How many candles did Lydia start with?

   _____

7. A coin purse contains quarters, dimes, and nickels. There are the same number of dimes as nickels and half as many quarters as dimes. The coins are worth $1.65. How many of each coin are in the coin purse?

   _____

8. The sum of two numbers is 20. The greater number is 4 more than the lesser number. What are the two numbers?

   _____

9. A garage charged Mr. Tilton $48 in parts and $36/h in labor. How many hours did the garage spend on Mr. Tilton's car if the total bill was $156?

   _____

▬▬Practice 11-6 Translations

Use the graph at the right for Exercises 1–4.

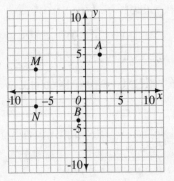

1. Give the coordinates of point A after it has been translated down 3 units. _____

2. Give the coordinates of point B after it has been translated left 3 units. _____

3. Suppose $M(-7, 3) \rightarrow M'(4, -1)$. What is the horizontal change? the vertical change? _____

4. What are the coordinates of point N after it is translated right 8 units and up 5 units? _____

Graph figure $ABCD$ and its image after each translation. Name the coordinates of A', B', C', and D'.

5. $A(2, 1)$, $B(4, 5)$, $C(7, 4)$, $D(5, -1)$; right 2 units

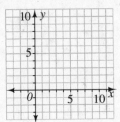

_____

6. $A(2, 1)$, $B(4, 5)$, $C(7, 4)$, $D(5, -1)$; down 1 unit, left 2 units

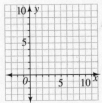

_____

Write the rule for the translation shown in each graph.

7.

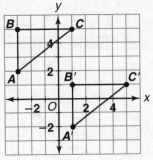

_____

8.

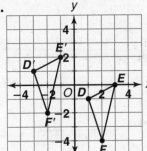

_____

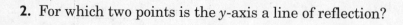

Practice 11-7 Symmetry and Reflections

Use the graph at the right for Exercises 1–3.

1. For which two points is the x-axis a line of reflection?

   _____

2. For which two points is the y-axis a line of reflection?

   _____

3. Points L and J are not reflections across the y-axis. Why not?

   _____

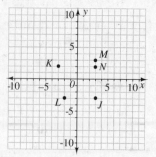

$\triangle A'B'C'$ **is a reflection of** $\triangle ABC$ **across the** x**-axis. Draw** $\triangle A'B'C'$ **and complete each statement.**

4. $A(-4, 1) \rightarrow A'(\blacksquare, \blacksquare)$ _____

5. $B(-1, 5) \rightarrow B'(\blacksquare, \blacksquare)$ _____

6. $C(6, 2) \rightarrow C'(\blacksquare, \blacksquare)$ _____

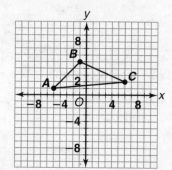

Draw the lines of symmetry of each figure. If there are none, write *none***.**

7.

8.

9.

10.

Use the graph at the right. Graph the image point for each reflection. Name the coordinates of the image point.

11. $(-3, 4)$ across the y-axis _____

12. $(-4, -2)$ across the x-axis _____

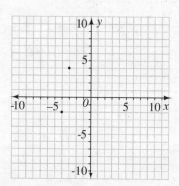

Practice 11-8 Rotations

Which figures have rotational symmetry? Explain.

1.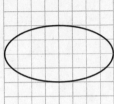

2.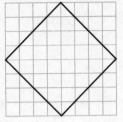

3.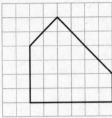

4.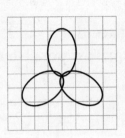

_____   _____   _____   _____

Draw the image of each figure after the given rotation about point _O_.

5. 90° rotation
6. 180° rotation
7. 270° rotation
8. 180° rotation

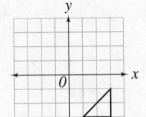   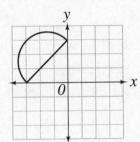   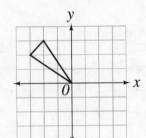   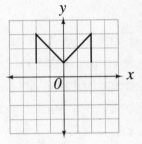

Figure II is the image of Figure I. Identify the transformation as a translation, a reflection, or a rotation.

9.

10.

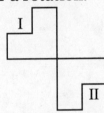

_____   _____

11.

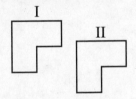

12.

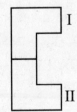

_____   _____

▬▬Enrichment: Minds on Math

1-1

Place the digits 2, 4, 5, 6, and 9 in the boxes to make the smallest possible difference.

☐☐☐
− ☐☐

1-2

Place one X in as many small squares as possible without forming a line of three Xs in a row either vertically, horizontally, or diagonally. What is the greatest number of Xs for which you can do this?

1-3

Holland Middle School is in a ten-team conference. During basketball season, each basketball team plays each other team at home. How many conference basketball games are played in a season?

Enrichment: Minds on Math

For Lessons 1-4 through 1-6

1-4

Of 100 students asked if they like rock-and-roll or country music, 7 said they like neither, 90 said they like rock-and-roll music, and 57 said they like country music. How many students like both?

1-5

Nine copies of a newsletter cost less than $10. Ten copies of the same newsletter at the same price cost more than $11. What is the cost of one newsletter?

1-6

I am the part of the set of whole numbers between 100 and 400 that contain the digit 2. How many whole numbers are in my set?

■■■■Enrichment: Minds on Math

For Lessons 1-7 through 1-9

1-7

When you multiply 2,178 by four, the product is 8,712. Notice that the digits in the product are the reverse of the digits in 2,178. Find the four-digit number whose digits are reversed when multiplied by nine.

1-8

During a twelve-hour period, the digit 1 shows up most often on a digital clock. Which digit shows up next to most often?

1-9

A store owner bought several boxes of denim shirts to sell at her store. The shirts cost her $6 each and come one dozen to a box. The third digit on the total on her receipt was missing. If the receipt read $12D84, where D is the missing digit, how many shirts did she buy?

◼◼ *Enrichment: Minds on Math* *For Lessons 2-1 through 2-3*

2-1

The number on Luke's locker has three digits. The middle digit is twice the first digit. The last digit is one less than the middle digit. The sum of the digits is 14. What is the number?

2-2

Marika called two of the members of her softball team to tell them their practice schedule for the week. Each of those team members called three other team members, and then each of those members called two more team members. How many team members were called? Do not include Marika.

2-3

Ulysses began with a number, multiplied his number by 2, divided the product by 5, and then added 9. The result was 19. With what number did Ulysses begin?

■■■■Enrichment: Minds on Math

2-4

Each girl in the Lynberg family has the same number of brothers as she has sisters. Each boy in the Lynberg family has twice as many sisters as he has brothers. How many girls and boys are there in the Lynberg family?

2-5

Six classmates are sitting at a rectangular table. Two are sitting along each long side. Stella and Troy are sitting at the short ends of the table. No girls are sitting next to each other. Melvin is at Dawnett's left. Ray is across from Melvin. Who is sitting at Diane's left?

2-6

Ted told Frank that all of the markers in Ted's box were black except for two, all were red except for two, and all were purple except for two. How many markers were in Ted's box?

Enrichment: Minds on Math

For Lessons 2-7 through 2-8

2-7

Tia has one less than twice the number of pets that Marcus has. Together they have 8 pets. How many pets does Marcus have?

2-8

Briton wants to place an even number of chairs along the walls in a rectangular room so that there are the same number of chairs along each wall. How can he do that? (Hint: a chair in a corner counts for two walls.)

■■■ Enrichment: Minds on Math   *For Lessons 3-1 through 3-3*

3-1

Lon, Jon, and Vaughn all live next to each other in three houses on the same street. Their houses are brown, white, and green. Lon does not live in the brown house. Vaughn's house is white and is next to Lon's house. Jon's house is next to the green house. What color is Lon's house? Where does Lon live in relationship to Jon and Vaughn?'

3-2

Janelle puts one piece of paper on top of another and cuts them both in half. She now has 4 pieces of paper. She stacks the pieces and cuts the stack in half to get 8 pieces of paper. Repeating this process, how many cuts will Janelle need to make in all to get 128 pieces of paper?

3-3

I am a three-digit number. The sum of my digits is 26. My last two digits are the same. What number am I?

Enrichment: Minds on Math   *For Lessons 3-4 through 3-6*

3-4

The counting numbers are arranged in a triangle array as begun below. In what row is the number 50?

```
        1
      2   3
    4   5   6
  7   8   9   10
```

3-5

Students from four classes of about the same size at Clinton Middle School are going on a tour of the historical center. The largest class going has 29 students. If the students divide into groups of 9 for the tour, there will be 2 students left over. If the students divide into groups of 15 for the tour, there will be 5 students left over. How many students are going on the tour?

3-6

Jamil planted half of the plants in his garden in rows of 18 and the other half of the plants in rows of 24. If he planted a total of 14 rows, how many plants are in his garden?

▬▬■*Enrichment: Minds on Math*   *For Lessons 3-7 through 3-10*

3-7

I am a three-digit number. I am exactly divisible by 24 and by 36. When I am divided by 24, the quotient is 6 more than the quotient when I am divided by 36. What number am I?

3-8

Kira is fertilizing her garden. She wants to add 2 tsp of fertilizer to 1 gal of water. She has a 3-gal bucket and a 7-gal bucket. How can she use these buckets to measure 1 gal of water?

3-9

Find the value of this expression.
$1 + 1 \times 1 \div 1 - 1 \div 1 + 1 \times (1 - 1) + 1$

3-10

Trevor has 8 square tables. One person can sit at each side of each table. Trevor wants to arrange the tables so that each table shares a side with at least one other table. He wants to be able to seat 18 people. How could Trevor arrange the tables? Find as many arrangements as you can.

▰ *Enrichment: Minds on Math*   *For Lessons 4-1 through 4-3*

4-1

Draw exactly four triangles to make the figure below.

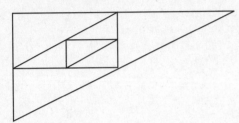

4-2

In the equations below, ☐ represents a two-digit number and △ represents a three-digit number. What numbers do they represent?

$$248 - \Box = \triangle$$

$$64 + \Box = \triangle$$

4-3

A worm is trying to crawl out of a 3-ft deep hole. If the worm crawls up 7 in. and then falls down 2 in. each hour, how many hours will it take the worm to crawl out of the hole?

▰▰▰▰ *Enrichment: Minds on Math*   *For Lessons 4-4 through 4-6*

4-4

Paulette has six marbles that are the same size. Five of her marbles weigh the same. The other marble is heavier than the rest. Hahn is trying to determine which marble is heavier than the rest by using a balance scale and only two weighings. How can he do this?

4-5

A drop of water drips from a leaky faucet every 8 seconds. It takes 6 drops to make a milliliter of water. How many liters drip from this faucet in a week?

4-6

A number is divided by 6. When 8 is added to the doubled quotient, the answer is 24. What is the number?

■■■ *Enrichment: Minds on Math*   *For Lessons 4-7 through 4-9*

4-7

Kirk's family drove 400 mi on the first day of their vacation. Each day after that they drove half the distance they drove the day before. Their total trip was 775 mi long. How long did it take them to make the trip?

4-8

Five friends are seated in a row at a concert. Shayla is sitting next to Suki. Sam is in the middle of the row and sitting next to Suki and Sari. Shar is sitting on the right end of the row. Who is sitting on the left end of the row?

4-9

I am an integer 28 units from my opposite value on the number line. I am not 14. What integer am I?

Enrichment: Minds on Math

For Lessons 5-1 through 5-3

5-1

How many whole numbers that are made up of the digits 1, 2, 3, 4, and 5, each used at most once, are multiples of 8?

5-2

Show how a square could have one of the points below on each of its sides without touching the rectangle.

5-3

Write the numbers 2, 3, 4, 5, 6, 7, 8, 9, and 10 in the squares, using each number only once, so that the numbers in the squares on each of the four circles have a sum of 27.

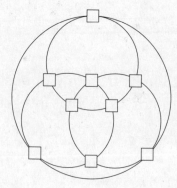

Enrichment: Minds on Math

For Lessons 5-4 through 5-6

5-4

What will row 50 of the pattern below look like?

$$1 + 2 = 3$$
$$4 + 5 + 6 = 7 + 8$$
$$9 + 10 + 11 + 12 = 13 + 14 + 15$$
$$16 + 17 + 18 + 19 + 20 = 21 + 22 + 23 + 24$$

5-5

I am a fraction in simplest form. I am greater than $\frac{1}{3}$ and less than $\frac{1}{2}$. The sum of all of my digits is 8. The difference between my numerator and denominator is 7. What fraction am I?

5-6

I am a two-digit number. My square is a number with its first two digits identical and its last two digits identical. What number am I?

Enrichment: Minds on Math
For Lessons 5-7 through 5-9

5-7

A gross is a dozen dozen. A great gross is a dozen gross.
How many objects are in a great gross?

5-8

Place the digits 2, 4, 5, and 7 in the boxes to make the
equation true.

$$\frac{3}{6} = \frac{9}{18} = \frac{\square\square}{\square\square}$$

5-9

Cameron invited 17 friends to his party. He assigned each
friend an integer from 2 to 18 and kept the number 1 for
himself. During one dance, everyone was dancing with a
partner. Cameron noticed that the sum of each couple's
numbers was a perfect square. What was Cameron's
partner's number during this dance?

Enrichment: Minds on Math

6-1

Take nine toothpicks and form this pattern. Move three toothpicks and make five triangles.

6-2

How can you use one 2 and one 6 to make 64?

6-3

If it takes Evelyn one minute to cut one board, how long will it take her to cut a 10-ft long board into 10 equal pieces?

■ ■ *Enrichment: Minds on Math*   *For Lessons 6-4 through 6-7*

6-4

Two bricks have the same weight. One brick is cut into quarters. The whole brick is then placed on one side of a scale. Three-fourths of the other brick is placed on the other side of the scale along with a 3–4-lb weight to balance the scale. How much did each brick weigh?

6-5

Use the pattern in the equations below to find the sum of the first 100 odd numbers.
$1 = 1$
$1 + 3 = 4$
$1 + 3 + 5 = 9$
$1 + 3 + 5 + 7 = 16$
$1 + 3 + 5 + 7 + 9 = 25$

6-6

Cameron has twice as many books as Kathi. Morey has one-third as many as Kira. Kira has 4 more books than Cameron. If Kathi has 16 books, how many books does Morey have?

6-7

Use a whole number, a fraction, one plus sign, and four 2's to make 23.

▰▰ *Enrichment: Minds on Math* For Lessons 6-8 through 6-11

6-8

A father wants to give some land to his three children. He gives $\frac{1}{2}$ of the land to the oldest child, $\frac{1}{3}$ of the land to his second child, $\frac{1}{9}$ of the land to his youngest child. Then he keeps 1 acre for himself. How many acres of land does each child get?

6-9

I am a 2-digit number. I am the difference of two numbers whose sum is 36. The larger of these numbers is twice the smaller. What number am I?

6-10

How many different squares are shown in the figure below?

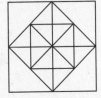

6-11

Fill in the boxes with the numbers 1 through 10 so that the number below any two numbers is the difference of those numbers. The order in which the numbers are subtracted does not have to be the same in each case.

Enrichment: Minds on Math

7-1

How many different triangles can you find in the figure?

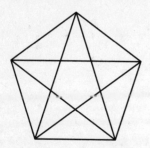

7-2

I am a three-digit number. When you reverse my digits, a larger number is formed. The product of me and the new number is 65,125. What number am I?

7-3

I am a two-digit odd number. My cube is a five-digit number. The digits in my cube are all different and are also different from my digits. What number am I?

Enrichment: Minds on Math

7-4

I am an acute angle. My supplement and my complement are themselves supplementary angles. What's my measure?

7-5

Points W, X, Y, and Z lie on the same line. Z is the point farthest to the left. If $XY = 5$, $XZ = 2$, and $XW = 6$, what is YW?

7-6

I am a seven-digit number. My first 5 digits are 2, 1, 3, 5, and 8 in that order. I am divisible by 99. What are my last two digits?

▰ *Enrichment: Minds on Math*   *For Lessons 7-7 through 7-9*

7-7

Angie and Tim drew different angles. The measure of Angie's angle is 2 more than 3 times the measure of Tim's angle. Angie's angle is 26° larger than a right angle. What is the measure of Tim's angle?

7-8

Use 3 segments to divide the equilateral triangle below into 4 congruent triangles.

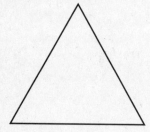

7-9

How would you divide the figure below into two congruent parts?

Enrichment: Minds on Math

8-1

Jena, Sally, Jack, and Gary have seats next to each other at a play. Jack sits next to Sally but not next to Gary. Gary is not sitting next to Jena. Who is sitting next to Jena?

8-2

One of the players on the Jenks High School football team tells his friend that all of the numbers on their jerseys are prime numbers less than 100. What is the greatest number of players that can be on the team?

8-3

The students in Miss Kirk's dance class stand evenly spaced in a circle. The students count off by 1s. The student who counts a 6 is directly across from the student who counts 19. How many students are in Miss Kirk's class?

▪ *Enrichment: Minds on Math*   For Lessons 8-4 through 8-7

8-4

What is the total number of triangles
in the figure?

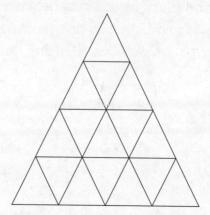

8-5

There are fewer sixth-grade students than seventh-grade
students in the Rice School District. The ninth grade has
more students than either the eighth grade or the seventh
grade. The number of students in the fifth grade is less
than the number in the sixth grade. Which of grades 5–9
has the most students?

8-6

Tia's softball uniform number has 2 digits and is a multiple
of 2, 4, 8, and 9. What is Tia's number?

8-7

If Lori gives Cameron 5 cookies, he will have 3 times as
many cookies as Lori. If Cameron gives Lori 5 cookies,
they will have the same number of cookies. How many
cookies do they each have?

■ *Enrichment: Minds on Math*   *For Lessons 8-8 through 8-11*

8-8

Find the length x of the side of the triangle below.

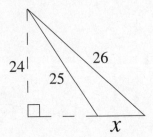

8-9

The lengths of the sides of a right triangle are consecutive whole numbers. What is the area of the triangle?

8-10

One fourth of one third is the same as one half of what fraction?

8-11

The diagonal of a rectangle has length $\sqrt{40}$ m. The area of the rectangle is 12 m^2. What is the perimeter of the rectangle?

Enrichment: Minds on Math
For Lessons 9-1 through 9-3

9-1

A class of 22 students wants to break into small groups of different sizes. No two groups can have the same number of students. What is the greatest number of groups they could form? What are the sizes of these groups?

9-2

Henry used $\frac{1}{2}$ of his flour to make blueberry muffins and $\frac{1}{2}$ of the remaining flour to make bran muffins. He has $1\frac{1}{2}$ c of flour left. How much flour did he start with?

9-3

Shauna is half as old as Tatum. In twelve years, Shauna will be $\frac{5}{8}$ as old as Tatum. How old is Tatum now?

Enrichment: Minds on Math
For Lessons 9-4 through 9-6

9-4

I am a percent. The sum of my digits is 15. I have three digits and a decimal point. I am less than 100%. I am equal to a fraction in simplest form. The fraction in simplest form has a denominator that is a multiple of 4 and less than 10. What percent am I?

9-5

What is the relationship between the radius of each circle and the sides of the rectangle?

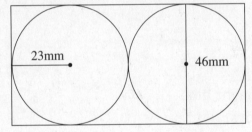

9-6

Kahlil, Juan, Waylon, and Ricki all bought identical T-shirts. Kahlil paid 10% more than Juan. Juan paid one fourth of what Waylon paid. Ricki paid 50% less than Waylon. Who paid the most? Who paid the least?

◼◼◼Enrichment: Minds on Math

For Lessons 9-7 through 9-8

9-7

We are three different unit fractions that add to 1. What unit fractions are we?

9-8

In April, 20% of the customers at Auto World bought blue cars. Of those customers, 15% chose gray interiors. What percent of the customers at Auto World did not choose a blue car with a gray interior?

▬ Enrichment: Minds on Math   *For Lessons 10-1 through 10-3*

10-1

Misty is sharing some cookies with three of her friends. She gives half of the cookies plus half a cookie to Lisa. She then gives half of the cookies left plus half a cookie to Laura. Finally she gives half of what is left and half a cookie to Lani. Misty says that she has given away all of her cookies without cutting, breaking, or dividing any of the cookies. How many cookies did Misty have at the beginning?

10-2

I am a mixed number less than 10. When I am divided by 4, the result is the same as when 4 is subtracted from me. What mixed number am I?

10-3

I am a polygon. When either one of my two diagonals are drawn, I am divided into 2 congruent triangles. What kind of polygon must I be?

■■■■ Enrichment: Minds on Math *For Lessons 10-4 through 10-5*

10-4

Jacalyn asked her friends to guess the number of buttons in a jar. Three of her friends guessed 495, 514, and 537. One of the guesses was off by 8, another by 15, and another by 27. How many buttons were in the jar?

10-5

There are a total of 12 cards of four colors in a box. The probability of drawing a green card is the same as the probability of drawing a yellow card. The probability of drawing a red card is $\frac{1}{4}$. The probability of drawing a blue card is $\frac{1}{12}$. How many green cards are in the box?

Enrichment: Minds on Math

For Lessons 10-6 through 10-7

10-6

I am a four-digit number. All of my digits are different, and none is a zero. The last digit is twice the first digit. The second digit is 3 less than the third digit. The sum of the first digit and the last digit is equal to the third digit. What number am I?

10-7

Write the numbers 1 through 10 in the rectangles so that the three numbers across the top or bottom as well as the four numbers down each side total 18.

■■ Enrichment: Minds on Math *For Lessons 11-1 through 11-3*

11-1

Judy listed a fifth number with the set of data 3, 6, 7, 10. The number she included made the mean of the five numbers equal to their median. What number could Judy have included with the data?

11-2

Kerri, Cassi, and Sam run laps every day after school. Kerri runs $\frac{1}{3}$ of a lap per minute, Cassi runs $\frac{1}{5}$ of a lap per minute, and Sam runs $\frac{1}{6}$ of a lap per minute. They start running at the same place and agree to continue running until they reach the starting point at the same time. How many laps do they each run?

11-3

One year, there were exactly 4 Tuesdays and 4 Saturdays in October. On what day did October 1 fall that year?

Enrichment: Minds on Math *For Lessons 11-4 through 11-6*

11-4

Gregory arranged the numbers 2, 3, 4, and 5, one plus sign, and one equals sign into a true equation. Show how Gregory might have done this.

11-5

A survey of 40 shoppers found that 12 liked Crunchy Cereal and 23 liked Wheat Bran Cereal. Twice as many disliked both brands as liked both brands. How many shoppers liked both brands?

11-6

In the first 3 games of this basketball season, Trisha made 12 of 30 shots. In her next game, she took 10 shots and raised her season average to 50%. How many of the 10 shots did she make?

▬▬▬ *Enrichment: Minds on Math* For Lessons 11-7 through 11-8

11-7

Shauna and Tatum are making marshmallow treats for camp. Their recipe calls for a total of 160 ounces of marshmallows. Marshmallows come in 16-ounce, 24-ounce, and 36-ounce bags. How many different combinations of bags could they use so that they would not have any left over?

11-8

A car has wheels with a diameter of 3 ft. About how many miles per hour is the car traveling if the wheels are turning about 600 times a minute?